C000244373

# GREAT WORLD WONDERS

## 100 remarkable World Heritage Sites

---

## Michael Turtle

Aboriginal and Torres Strait Islander readers are advised that this book may contain names of people who have died.

Hardie Grant

TRAVEL

# Contents

## 01

### HOMES OF THE RICH AND FAMOUS

## 02

### AT THE MOVIES

## 03

### A TALE OF TWELVE CITIES

# 05

## STATES OF
## THE ARTS

# 04

## ON FAITH
## VALUE

# 06

## WHO, WHEN,
## WHERE?

# 08

## SCIENCE AND TECHNOLOGY

# 07

## THE NATURAL WORLD

# 09

## HISTORY'S GREAT EMPIRES

# 10

## LOVE AT
## FIRST SITE

# Introduction

Waiting on the roadside in a small Chilean city, probably the only foreigner for miles, I wondered if this was all worth it. Tourists don't come to Rancagua. I was only there to meet a guide I had found online after hours of research (and after stretching my terrible Spanish to its limits). This was the only possible way to go the next 60 kilometres (37 miles) up into the Andes – through locked gates and along treacherous cliffside roads – to the abandoned mining town of Sewell (*see* p. 210).

Once I arrived, any thoughts that this was a waste of time evaporated. I found an incredible town painted a rainbow of colours by miners living in desolate conditions, preserved perfectly in the mountains, empty but for our little tour group walking through the time capsules of buildings. Despite the difficulties, taking the time for this visit was not just worth it, it was a highlight of my trip in Chile. And the only reason I had decided to come in the first place? Because Sewell is a UNESCO World Heritage Site ... and I had pledged to visit them all.

There are more than 1100 UNESCO World Heritage Sites and about 20 new ones are added each year. My aim to visit every one, even I admit, is probably unattainable – especially when you consider that some are so remote or protected that they're impossible to get to. (There's even a World Heritage Site belonging to the UK actually called Inaccessible Islands!) But it's not crossing the sites off my travel list that is the appeal. It's using them to learn more about a country, to discover the shared humanity we have, and ultimately to understand the world.

I like to think of the World Heritage List as a museum of places. If you could put together a collection of all the sites in the world that tell the story of our planet – natural and cultural – then that's what it is. The best examples of architectural style, major civilisations, of natural ecosystems, of every faith, royal dynasty and industry-changing invention, and everything that makes us who we are. If you think about it like that, it is the greatest museum you could ever curate, and just exploring one of its wings should be enough for a lifetime.

There are occasions when I visit a country and plan an itinerary that takes me to all of its World Heritage Sites. It always gives me a remarkable insight into the nation's story, often leading me through each of the most significant historical eras and cultural movements. I remember the Czech Republic, for instance, which took me to Prague, of course, but also the small rural village of Holašovice, and then the modernist Villa Tugendhat in Brno, providing a wide spectrum of culture. There are always sites that I have never heard of (sometimes many) but most of them are fascinating and, in their own ways, beautiful. I'll come away thankful I've seen them and curious as to why they are not visited by more travellers.

My pursuit of World Heritage Sites also provides some of my most memorable travel experiences – walking amongst prehistoric killer reptiles in Indonesia, horseriding for days through the mountains of Kyrgyzstan, discovering ancient soaring temples in Mexico's jungle, and even drinking wine overlooking the green hills of France. It started as a list of destinations, but it's turned into the most rewarding of journeys. But that's often what you find when you travel with an interest in the world.

In this book, I share with you 100 sites that I've chosen as a good representation of the marvels on the World Heritage List – a quick tour of this incredible museum of places. Each chapter covers a particular theme, looking at the opulent homes of historical figures, or the beating hearts of some of history's great empires. There are chapters dedicated to art, to science, and to faith. And I will take you from some of the busiest cities to some of the most remote natural wonders.

Each site has many stories to tell – sometimes ones that change shape from different perspectives or have evolved with the lucidity of time. But, as much as possible, I have tried to let these wonders of the world speak for themselves.

*Michael Turtle*

**Time Travel Turtle**
timetravelturtle.com

Iguazu Falls comprises natural World
Heritage Sites in Argentina and Brazil

# What is a World Heritage Site?

**When the UNESCO World Heritage List
was launched in 1978, it had just 12 sites.
Since then, it has grown to more than
1100 sites, but the work to get to this
point has not been simple (or without
controversy, as I mention in this book).**

There are three types of World Heritage
Sites – cultural (78 per cent), natural
(19 per cent), and a mix of cultural and
natural (3 per cent). To be added to the
list (inscribed) they need to satisfy at
least one of ten criteria, which include
'represent a masterpiece of human
creative genius', 'bear a unique or at
least exceptional testimony to a cultural

tradition', and 'contain the most important
and significant natural habitats for in-situ
conservation of biological diversity'.

Ultimately, what the criteria are trying
to determine is whether a site is of
'outstanding universal value', a phrase that
is interpreted differently by people, but
essentially means it is important beyond
its border and time period.

It's important to understand that, although
UNESCO is the caretaker of the list, it
doesn't just choose the sites it thinks
should be inscribed. A World Heritage
Site can only be nominated by the country

where it's located (with one exception granted for the Old City of Jerusalem, *see* p. 86, because of disagreement on which nation it belongs to). And then there's a long bureaucratic process that takes place.

The first step is for a country to officially place a site on what's called the Tentative List – and there are currently hundreds that have been added to that list over the decades but went no further. When the country decides it wants to advance the nomination, a years-long assessment period begins and independent advisory bodies compile a report with a recommendation of whether a site should be added or not. That report is then presented at an annual meeting of the World Heritage Committee (a revolving group of 21 countries), which votes on whether to inscribe the proposed site.

Although we officially call it a 'World Heritage Site', the title can be a bit misleading because the site can sometimes consist of multiple locations. For example, one called 'Rock Art of the Mediterranean Basin on the Iberian Peninsula' is actually made up of 758 different places across Spain! And a World Heritage Site can even be spread across countries or continents. One site that's a collection of architecture by Le Corbusier has locations in Argentina, Belgium, France, Germany, India, Japan, and Switzerland.

In the decades since 1978, the World Heritage List has added not just some of the world's most prominent landmarks, but lesser-known places linked by themes from the Silk Road to Art Deco architecture. The bureaucracy can be cumbersome, the process has often tended to favour European and wealthier countries, and there are legitimate questions about how issues like colonialism and conflict are portrayed. But ultimately there's a universal aim to protect and promote the best of our world.

## Inscribed

Each entry heading includes the year the site was officially inscribed as a UNESCO World Heritage Site. I've included 2 entries that were part of the first 12 UNESCO site list added in 1978 (Galápagos Islands, *see* p. 140, and Wieliczka Salt Mine, *see* p. 196). The newest sites featured in this book were inscribed in 2019 (Jaipur, *see* p. 68, Bagan, *see* p. 88, Vatnajökull National Park, *see* p. 190, Jodrell Bank Observatory *see* p. 198, and Budj Bim, *see* p. 218).

# Where in the world?

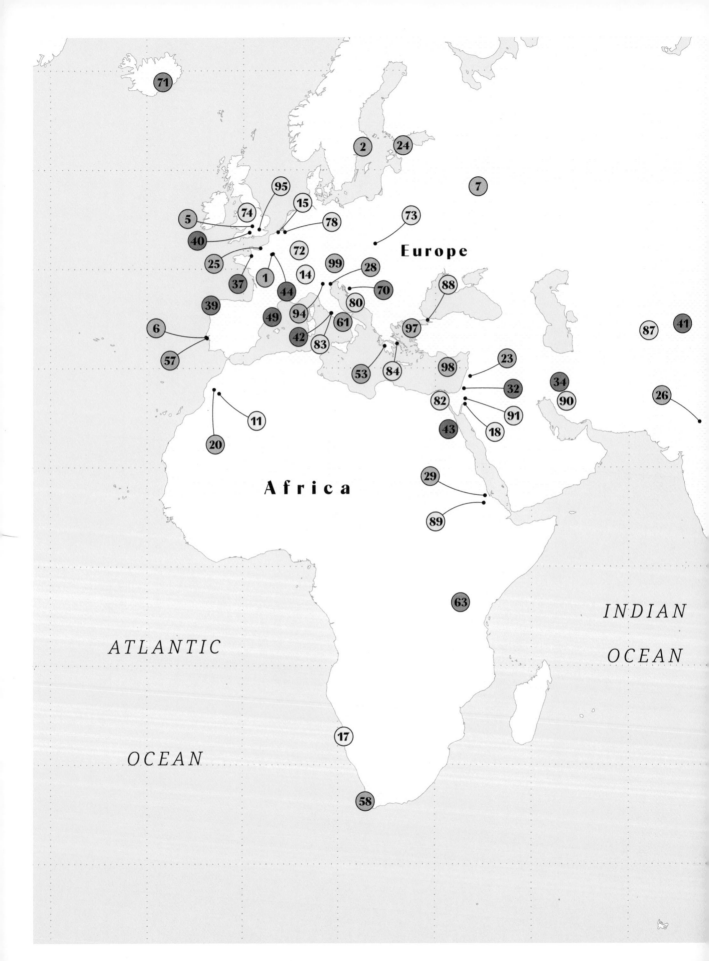

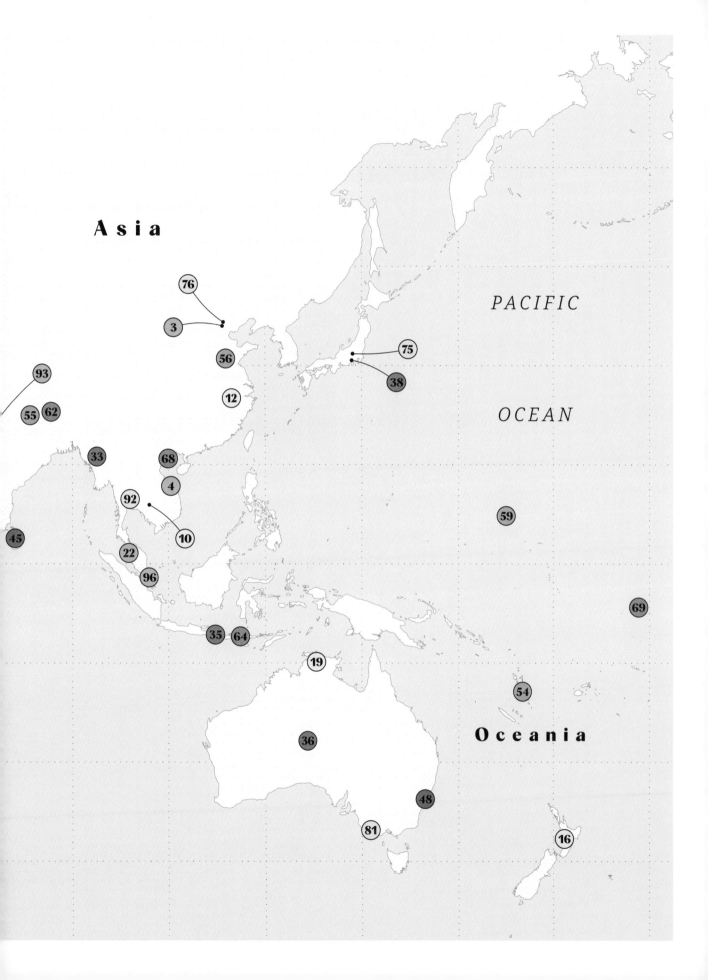

Asia

PACIFIC

OCEAN

Oceania

# Homes of the rich and famous

Why are we so fascinated with the grand homes of aristocrats and royalty? Is it curiosity about their lives, or is it because of the dazzling opulence of the palaces that we marvel at the munificent rooms and magnificent decorations? If it's the latter, the mansions and palaces are doing their job – because they were often built primarily to project power and prestige. More than residences, they were status symbols, sending messages to subjects and rivals alike.

From the Palace of Versailles in France (*see* p. 2) with its 2300 rooms, to the Forbidden City in China (*see* p. 6) that had space for 100,000 spectators at ceremonies, some of the most beautiful and interesting homes are now UNESCO World Heritage Sites. And, on occasion, we do get to peek through the curtains and see into the lives of some of history's characters. At US President Thomas Jefferson's Monticello home (*see* p. 20), we see the quarters where he kept his slaves; and at England's Blenheim Palace (*see* p. 12), we discover the childhood of Prime Minister Winston Churchill.

Whether they are royal palaces, aristocratic estates, or even small private homes, these residences push the boundaries of architectural and artistic styles. The best examples don't just dazzle in isolation, they begin movements that influence the way our world has been built.

01

# The Palace of Versailles

### *France* (Inscribed 1979)

Home to the French kings from 1682 until the French Revolution in 1789, the Palace of Versailles radiates with all the opulence you would expect from European royalty. It is a symbol of the biggest, most ornate, most luxurious and ostentatious display of power. There have been impressive attempts at emulating it, but nobody has ever created a more iconic royal residence.

The palace has 2300 rooms, including the state apartments with marble panelling and painted ceilings, the golden private bedrooms, a large gothic chapel, and even an opera house. The most famous feature is the Hall of Mirrors, a long bright room with twinkling chandeliers and 357 mirrors catching every move. It has seen emperors proclaimed, empires taken away, and empires redistributed – and even the mirrors themselves reflect spilled blood and boiling jealousies.

When the Palace of Versailles was being built, it was decided everything would be made in France ... except Venice had a monopoly on the manufacturing of mirrors. Artisans who had previously tried to take their secrets to other countries had been assassinated by the Venetian Government, but the French convinced a couple to defect and eventually, despite a campaign of threats of retribution, the mirrors for the hall could be made locally.

The whole palace is a bit like the Hall of Mirrors. At first it's the scale and the lavishness that awes you but, when you take the time to look closer, it's the details that are so impressive: Louis XV's astronomical clock that sits on a mantlepiece, the ornately carved crimson and gold chairs in the games room, the depictions of Greek mythology that follow you through the rooms. The first thing you notice about the Gallery of Great Battles, for example, is its length – at 120 metres (394 feet), it takes up the entire first floor of the south wing – but each of the 30 paintings on the wall of famous military successes could lead you down an even longer story.

So perhaps it's no surprise that Queen Marie Antoinette, one of the building's most famous residents, needed to often escape from the intimidation of the palace (even though she herself had grown up in Vienna's 1441-room Schönbrunn Palace, *see* p. 37). One of her favourite retreats was the Petit Trianon, a small chateau in the park. Marie Antoinette eventually expanded the gardens of the Petit

Trianon and built a model village around an artificial lake, leaving more of a mark at Versailles than any other queen. (You might say she was ahead of her time, although the time took her head.)

Both the Gardens and the Park of Versailles are integral to the design of the site, creating a natural visual flow between the interior and exterior. Too often I hear of visitors who only see the palace and skip the beautiful landscaping around it. But that would be a shame. The gardens took 40 years to create, designed and overseen by André Le Nôtre, with whole army regiments working on them, and every detail reviewed by King Louis XIV 'the Sun King' himself. There are formal gardens, 1400 fountains, a canal, orangerie and parklands. There's a reason nobody has ever built anything better.

**01.** The halls of the Palace of Versailles are decorated with sculptures and opulent colours **02.** The Hall of Mirrors was used daily by people waiting and meeting, and was only occasionally the venue for official ceremonies **03.** The Gardens of Versailles make up much of the 800 hectares (2000 acres) of the estate

# Drottningholm Palace

## *Sweden* (Inscribed 1991)

As I am walking around the public areas of Drottningholm Palace, one of the officials points at a closed door with a velvet rope in front of it. 'If you were to go and knock on that door,' he tells me, 'the king might answer. That's his study.'

It's unusual to have this kind of access to the home of a country's head of state. Even when you can visit royal residences, there's normally a stricter division between the public and the private than a door and a rope. But it seems the King and Queen of Sweden are rather laidback ... now.

But at the end of the 17th century, Sweden was trying to project an image as one of Europe's mightiest countries and Drottningholm Palace was part of that. It was one of the first grand royal residences inspired by France's Palace of Versailles (*see* p. 2), built at almost exactly the same time, with large lavish gardens and grand receptions halls. It was only later that the palace became more about culture than politics.

Drottningholm Palace was not the primary residence of the Swedish monarch until 1981. Before that, it was used as a summer palace or as the home for minor royals, many of whom embraced the arts and invited painters, poets, and philosophers to spend time here. The beautifully decorated library with playful Rococo ornamentation is testament to this. But the two most important remnants of this embrace of culture are the palace's Chinese Pavilion and its theatre.

**01.**

**01.** The Library of Queen Lovisa Ulrika was a meeting place for intellectuals and is considered one of the most beautiful rooms in Sweden **02.** The Chinese Pavilion in the gardens of Drottningholm Palace **03.** The Royal Family often travels from central Stockholm to Drottningholm Palace by boat

You'll find the Chinese Pavilion deep in the large gardens, at the end of an avenue of chestnut trees. Designed in the fashionable Chinese style of the day and filled with decorative items like porcelain, lacquered screens and silk, it tried to capture the exoticism of the East in the 18th century.

The theatre is next to the palace and was used for the premieres of European operas and other dramatic performances. It's one of the few theatres from the 18th century that has its original stage machinery (one of the reasons Drottningholm is a World Heritage Site), and you can still go to performances today. Sometimes the king and queen even attend ... not that it's a long walk for them.

# It was only later that the palace became more about culture than politics.

# The Forbidden City

## *China* (Inscribed 1987)

The Forbidden City dominates the heart of Beijing, an enormous complex of historical palaces, ceremonial buildings, and administrative areas that is a vestige of tradition at the geographical centre of the modern metropolis. About a kilometre on every side and surrounded by a wide moat, the fate of China was controlled from here for almost 500 years, behind high walls that protected the secrecy and mystique of imperial life. The Forbidden City saw 24 consecutive rulers of the Ming and Qing dynasties from 1416 until 1911.

The name of the Forbidden City is not just a trivial moniker. Apart from the fact it did operate like its own little city, it was also forbidden for most people to visit. Those who were allowed in, even imperial family members, were restricted to certain areas. Only the emperor himself could go wherever he wanted.

These days, visitors actually enter through the gate that was reserved for just the emperor. Known as the Meridian Gate, it is 38 metres high (124 feet) and has wings on either side that resemble the outstretched paws of a lion. (Not to be confused with the Gate of Heavenly Peace, the iconic façade with the painting of Mao Zedong, which is the entrance to the broader Imperial City that surrounded the more important Forbidden City.)

Beyond the Meridian Gate, over five marble bridges that cross a river running through the city, and through another gate, is the vast Outer Court. This open space could hold up to 100,000 people to watch what was happening in the centre, where a three-layered terrace supports three official buildings used for ceremonies like coronations and banquets. Beyond that is the Inner Court, the more private sanctum, with living quarters and rooms for daily governing. Along the two sides of the city were mazes of alleys and tiny courtyards, connecting administrative buildings, more residences, and halls used as reception rooms, galleries, and for minor ceremonies.

The Forbidden City was designed with the principles of feng shui and Confucianism, and the layout is full of symbolism and deeper meanings – odd numbers of things at the front and even numbers at the back, for instance. It would take more than a day to walk through and find all these details, but it's worth looking

for the animal decorations throughout, with dragons representing the omnipotence of the emperor, while birds and flowers were used to illustrate areas used by women, like the empress and the concubines. There were intentionally no trees in the large courts, encouraging people to prepare mentally before an important meeting as they crossed the wide open space.

Yellow, which represented the earth, was the colour of the emperor and was only used for buildings where he would be – the exception being the library, which had a black roof representing water, with the hope it would protect the books from fire. And, of course, you'll see red everywhere in the city, from walls to columns, because it is the colour of power, wealth, and honour.

From within these secretive walls, the emperors changed the face of China, yet the incredible palace complex still reflects the classic heritage of the great empire.

**01.** Jingshan Park overlooks the Forbidden City from a hill created with dirt excavated for the palace complex's moat **02.** There are decorations with animal motifs throughout the Forbidden City **03.** The Hall of Supreme Harmony, the ceremonial centre of imperial power

# The Imperial City of Hue

## *Vietnam* (Inscribed 1993)

The locations for palaces are chosen for many reasons. Because they are in the centre of the city, for example, or they have defensive advantages, or even just because they offer a pleasant vista. I doubt many are chosen so they would be protected by dragons, tigers, and snakes – but that's the story of how the Imperial City of Hue was founded in Vietnam.

The site was chosen using geomancy, a form of divination that's said to find the hidden energy and meanings of the earth. In the case of Hue, the geomancers thought the hills on either side of the site represented a blue dragon and a white tiger, which would stop evil spirits entering, while the Perfume River flowing beside it resembled a snake.

Construction of the Imperial City began in 1804 under Emperor Gia Long, who had unified Vietnam into the geographical country it resembles today. He began the Nguyen Dynasty, which would be the last series of emperors to rule Vietnam – right up until the end of World War II (although for much of that time it was really a titular role, with the French actually in charge).

The Imperial City was part of the Citadel of Hue, a huge area protected by a moat and a 10-kilometre-long (6-mile) wall. Much of the citadel is now suburban but the main Imperial City, with its own moat and 2.5-kilometre-long (1.5-mile) wall, remains ... at least, the parts of it that weren't damaged during the First Indochina War and then the Vietnam War (called the American War by the Vietnamese). However, much has been rebuilt since then

**01.** Red doors open out to a large courtyard **02.** Each design element in the city has been carefully considered **03.** The Ngọ Môn (Meridian Gate), built in 1833, is the city's main entrance **04.** A pagoda in front of the destroyed Kien Trung Pavilion

and work is ongoing to restore it to more of its former glory.

And what a glory Hue's Imperial City must have been! It was modelled after Beijing's Forbidden City (*see* p. 6), but the style here is uniquely Vietnamese. The yellow-tiled roofs are topped with ornate sculptures of dragons; blinds are painted with faces that have eyes that seem to bore into you; gates have colourful animal motifs climbing over them; and interior walls are vibrant with red lacquer and gold trim.

Throughout the city, temples and pagodas stand amongst green lawns. The central palaces in the emperor's exclusive enclave reveal a decadent lifestyle for the ruler, his wives and his concubines – and even the eunuchs who served them. Through it all, and around it all, are the water features, the large trees, and the mountain views that led to the creation of this luxurious complex.

To find out more about Vietnam's emperors, you can also visit their tombs set along the Perfume River, all ornate imperial buildings in themselves.

# More than your garden variety

When we think of the famous palaces and grandiose homes around the world, we often first picture the magnificent buildings that have made them so iconic. It's only a bit later that our focus turns to the gardens around them.

For many of these homes, it's actually the gardens and grounds that are more impressive. Some of the sites have been added to the World Heritage List primarily because their parks and gardens have incredible landscaping that influenced other designs for centuries.

One of the most famous in the world is the **Royal Botanic Gardens at Kew** in England. Kew Palace, the smallest of the British royal palaces, is really an afterthought for the gardens, which contain the largest botanic collection in the world. Likewise, **Kroměříž Castle** in the Czech Republic has a much smaller flower garden within high walls, but it's considered to be one of the best 17th-century garden designs, blending Italian Renaissance and French Baroque styles.

In Kyoto, the many stunning palaces, shrines and temples are some of the iconic images of Japan, but they are also among the best examples of Japanese gardens, where water is used symbolically and even the smallest raking of pebbles can change the balance. In South Korea, at the **Changdeokgung Palace Complex**, the Joseon Dynasty laid out their buildings in harmony with the topography of a sacred mountain, creating a terraced garden that embraced the palace site.

The **Golestan Palace** in Iran's capital, Tehran, dazzles with coloured tiles that catch the sun, but the vibrancy is amplified in the surrounding garden as the buildings are reflected by the large pools. While in the Pakistani city of Lahore, the enormous **Shalimar Gardens** also use water features to add a sense of motion amongst the lawns and trees which, along with the **Lahore Fort**, are masterpieces of the Mughal civilisation.

## Some of the sites have been added to the World Heritage List primarily because their parks and gardens have incredible landscaping that influenced other designs for centuries.

Shalimar Gardens in Lahore, Pakistan **Inset** Royal Botanic Gardens at Kew, United Kingdom

# Blenheim Palace

### *United Kingdom* (Inscribed 1987)

There was a rumour that if Adolf Hitler ever successfully invaded England, he planned to make Blenheim Palace his official residence. Near Oxford, about 100 kilometres (62 miles) from London, it seems like an odd choice. But there was something significant, something personal, behind this plan. Blenheim Palace was the birthplace and childhood home of Winston Churchill, the British Prime Minister who was leading the war efforts against Hitler. For the Führer

to take it would be the ultimate insult to his adversary.

Of course, Hitler never got the chance and the palatial residence is still in the hands of the Duke of Marlborough, just like it was for the 11 Dukes of Marlborough before him. The land was gifted to the first duke in 1705 by Queen Anne as a reward for his military victory over the French and Bavarians at the Battle of Blenheim the year before. It's the only non-royal and non-religious house in England allowed to call itself a 'palace'.

Although it's a private house, it is enormous and is a rare example of English Baroque architecture, a style popularised by Christopher Wren. The palace has 187 rooms, including the soaring Great Hall with marble pillars and archways, the dining room covered in 18th-century wall paintings with a perfectly set table of crystal, china and silver in the centre, and the 55-metre-long (180-foot) library complete with an imposing organ at one end (which is presumably quite distracting if you're trying to read). Priceless artworks hang on the wall, but some of the most important are painted on the ceilings, like James Thornhill's depiction of the first Duke of Marlborough kneeling to Britannia.

All of this is expensive to maintain, and the family almost lost Blenheim Palace when the

estate neared bankruptcy at the end of the 1800s. But the 9th Duke of Marlborough, Charles Spencer-Churchill, saved the house by marrying American railroad heiress Consuelo Vanderbilt, who traded some of her family fortune for the title of Duchess. (The dowry was worth about US$80 million in today's terms.)

Along with the main building, the Blenheim Palace Park is also part of the World Heritage Site, its sprawling landscape designed by Lancelot 'Capability' Brown, often described as England's greatest gardener. With two artificial lakes, oak woodlands, and grassy expanses, it's considered a masterpiece that has influenced many royal gardens across Europe.

**01.** The grand North Portico is the main entrance to Blenheim Palace **02.** The Great Court, with Renaissance-style statues looking down from the rooftops **03.** Sculpture on display in the grounds. The Blenheim Art Foundation now collects both contemporary and classic art.

The South Lawn of Blenheim Palace is often used to host events

# Sintra

## *Portugal* (Inscribed 1995)

At the top of a lush green hill, a vermillion turret pokes out beyond the trees. Beneath that, a bright yellow castle is connected to a purple-tiled façade. Around it all is a low crenellated wall that is clearly more decorative than defensive – but that's no surprise. This is purely a pleasure palace.

Pena Palace was built (and painted so vibrantly) in the mid-19th century by the Portuguese Royal Family as a summer escape – the forested hills of Sintra are just 20 kilometres (12 miles) from Lisbon, but the temperature can be at least five degrees Celsius cooler. And they weren't the only ones to take advantage of this cool oasis. Many wealthy residents from the capital established homes here, taking inspiration for the designs from the Romanticism movement that was about to sweep Europe.

With bright colours, playful artistic embellishments, and quirky landscaping, the town of Sintra and its surrounding hills were transformed into a playground, most of which is now the World Heritage Site. The best example is Quinta da Regaleira, a 4 hectare (10 acre) estate that was developed by a rich businessman with a palace at its centre and a garden full of strange features referencing things like the Knights Templar and the Masons. There's even a mysterious 27-metre-deep (88.5-foot) well with a spiral staircase you can walk down that leads to hidden tunnels at the bottom.

But going down the well and emerging from these weird underground passages, it's as though Alice took a wrong turn and ended up in Narnia, rather than Wonderland. Because before Sintra was a kingdom of Romanticism, it was the scene of constant conflict between Moors and Christians and the region changed hands back and forth. The Moorish Castle, built in the 10th century with sweeping views, was part of a fortification system and you can still walk along the sturdy stone walls of its ruins. Its medieval towers rising amongst the forest only add to the intriguing romance of the landscape.

Well after the battles finished, the first proper palace was built at Sintra in the 15th century when the Portuguese kings first began to holiday here. The National Palace is from this time, and it's easy to spot with two enormous white chimneys that look like factory smoke

stacks rising up from the roof. Inside, many of the rooms are decorated with murals and ornate mosaic tiled walls, similar to the traditional styles you'll find across Portugal.

The National Palace, now a museum, may not have the flamboyant colours of the Pena Palace but it began the movement of the rich and famous holidaying here as a refuge from the city. Today, there are still dozens of private houses in the hills, hidden behind gates, that you can steal glimpses of as you make your way up the narrow winding roads of this fairytale wonderland.

**01.** The Sintra region is characterised by colourful buildings set amongst lush green hills **02.** Visitors can walk along the fortified walls of the Moorish Castle **03.** The vibrant Pena Palace was built in the mid-19th century

# The Kremlin

## *Russia* (Inscribed 1990)

Although we may think of it as a name, a proper noun, Russia's most famous site is actually originally just a common noun. The word kremlin means a fortified central complex within a city – and there are quite a few of them in Russia. It just goes to show how important the Moscow one is that it is simply called THE Kremlin.

These days, just the name can conjure up a sense of infamy because of movie depictions of it as a centre of espionage and global conspiracies. That perception (real or not) is probably a bit of a hangover from the Soviet era when it was quite an exclusive enclave for the ruling elite. But just like at the White House in Washington or the Élysée Palace in Paris, much of what happens at the official residence of the Russian president is presumably rather mundane living and governing.

But what makes the Kremlin different to many other presidential palaces around the world is that it's not solely a residence and office. The complex is huge, with a 2.2 kilometre (1.3 mile) wall around the site, and multiple palaces and cathedrals. And, demystifying the site, much of it is now open to the public, with some of the buildings turned into museums. Of note is the Armoury, a treasure trove of more than 4000 items that includes royal thrones, crowns, and Fabergé eggs ... oh, and lots of armour.

The museum's collection reflects the long and auspicious history of the Kremlin, which has existed in some form since 1156. It has been the centre of the Russian Orthodox Church, home to the country's most famous tsars, and the heart of the government during the imperial period and then the Soviet era. Oh, if these walls could talk!

01

Speaking of walls, the exterior defensive wall, with four gates and 20 towers, is also considered to be one of the most significant constructions at the site. Just below the ramparts on the eastern side is the iconic St Basil's Cathedral, with its colourful onion-shaped domes that look like candy. The cathedral is on Red Square, which connects to the Kremlin and is also part of the World Heritage Site.

Red Square, along with St Basil's Cathedral and the Kremlin are geographically at the centre of Moscow – and politically, culturally, and even spiritually, they have been central to the story of Russia for centuries.

**01.** The Hall of the Order of St Andrew in the Grand Kremlin Palace was used as a throne room **02.** A large red wall runs the entire length of the Kremlin's boundary **03.** The clocks on Spasskaya Tower, known as the Kremlin Chimes, officially ring in the new year in Moscow

(01)

# Monticello

## *United States of America* (Inscribed 1987)

When it comes to the creations of Thomas Jefferson, he is probably best known for the Declaration of Independence, with its stirring words of the unalienable rights of 'life, liberty, and the pursuit of happiness'. But Jefferson was a complex character – not just for the moral contradictions that arise from being a slave-owner. He was also renowned as an architect, with his own house, called Monticello, another of his famous creations.

Monticello, at the top of a small hill within a wooded estate in Virginia, was listed as a World Heritage Site partly because it's an

excellent example of Neoclassical architecture. But there's obviously much more to it than that. You can't separate Jefferson's design from the fact that he was doing much of it while he was also vice-president and president at the beginning of the 1800s. Taking influence from his time in Europe, the style reflected the ideals of Ancient Rome that he believed his newborn country should also have – freedom, nobility, and self-determination.

Of course, the idea of self-determination now seems relative when we discuss the legacy of Thomas Jefferson. Even though he wrote in the Declaration of Independence that 'all men are created equal', he owned about 600 slaves during his lifetime, most of them working on his plantations and in his household. The slaves were accommodated in two pavilions, stretching out as wings from either side of the main house and hidden under open-air terraces. The slave quarters were also where they worked and were connected by tunnels so they could come up into different parts of the house.

In the main house, Jefferson designed many architectural quirks, including an eight-sided guest room, a bedroom that saved space by having the bed in an alcove, and the distinctive dome that rises from the centre of the building.

For almost a century after Jefferson's death, Monticello changed hands, being sold, inherited, and even seized by the Confederacy at one point. But since 1923 it has been maintained as a museum. Thomas Jefferson is buried on the grounds.

Even though he wrote in the Declaration of Independence that 'all men are created equal', he owned about 600 slaves during his lifetime.

01. The kitchen in the slave quarters of Monticello, out of sight of the main part of the house 02. Despite declaring 'all men are created equal', Thomas Jefferson had a controversial history with slavery 03. The design of Monticello was heavily influenced by architecture styles in Europe

# Sans-Souci Palace

## *Haiti* (Inscribed 1982)

It was supposed to be the Versailles of the Caribbean, but Sans-Souci Palace in Haiti was not 'without worries', as its French meaning may suggest. It was built from 1810 by the first (and, spoiler alert, only) King of Haiti, Henri Christophe. He was a former slave who became the president after the independence revolution against France and then named himself king. (The Haiti he ruled was only the northern half of the Haiti that we know today.)

The palace was grandiose, unlike anything seen before in the region. Set on a hill among the rainforest, it was about 60 metres (197 feet) long with large gardens and water features around it. It had a sumptuous dining room for lavish feasts, and terraces that guests would spill onto in the warm tropical evenings. In every sense, it would impress its visitors – which was the whole point.

But the problem was that the king was, by most accounts, a megalomaniac dictator. Hundreds, if not thousands, of labourers died while building Sans-Souci over the course of three years – and it was just one of nine palaces and 15 chateaux that he built. Although it's said that he wanted the grandeur of the palace to prove the greatness of the African descendants in the West Indies – one of the reasons he filled it with marble, mahogany and mosaics – he still treated many of his own subjects like slaves.

01

Yet, in Haiti today, he is celebrated as a symbol of independence and is featured on one of the country's banknotes.

After Henri Christophe died in 1820, and his son was assassinated 10 days later, the palace was looted, but the buildings survived until an earthquake in 1842. What you find today are the ruins, but still with enough glory to evoke images of its past. Walking through the entrance gates, into the halls, upstairs, to views across the green hills, you get a sense that this palatial complex was witness to the beginnings of a new independent country.

Sans-Souci and the other royal buildings in the area were the first government monuments in the world to be constructed by slaves who had gained their freedom. That the ruins still standing amongst the trees now look like a broken crown, a fitting symbol for the failed monarchy of a self-proclaimed king, is just part of the story.

# The palace was grandiose, unlike anything seen before in the region.

**01.** The main building of Sans-Souci Palace was intended to project a sense of power **02.** The original palace buildings haven't been restored since an earthquake in 1842 **03.** The stepped gardens of the palace were designed to be reminiscent of those in Potsdam or Vienna

# Homes of the less famous

While all of the homes highlighted in this chapter have been built for royals, the rich and the renowned, there are quite a few interesting examples of ordinary houses that have been made World Heritage Sites because they are actually quite special.

In the semi-mountainous region of **Koutammakou** in Togo, the Batammariba people live in remarkable cylindrical tower-houses of mud, topped with conical thatched roofs. The homes are usually two storeys high, the ground floor used to keep livestock at night, and the upper floor for sleeping and drying grain.

In Yemen, it is a different type of tower-house that makes the 16th-century city of **Shibam** significant. Made from sun-dried bricks, the apartment blocks are up to 30 metres (98 feet) high and are tightly packed together like skyscrapers. It's easy to see why Shibam has the nickname, 'Manhattan of the Desert'.

The **Fujian province** of China has some fascinating residential buildings called tulou, large communal living blocks several storeys high with thick earthen outer walls. Shaped as circles, or sometimes squares, they have a large central courtyard that each residence looks down into. Built between the 14th and 20th centuries, the largest ones are home to up to 800 people.

In the Chinese city of **Kaiping**, there's a completely different style called diaolou. These tall thin apartment blocks are from the 1920s and 1930s and look like castles. They are a fusion of Chinese and Western styles and were built by Chinese immigrants returning from places like North America and Hong Kong.

The trulli in the Italian town of **Alberobello** are a striking type of house, dry-wall huts of limestone with walls painted white and natural-coloured conical roofs. Built from the 14th century and connected to each other, there are more than a thousand lining the streets.

And then there are the gorgeous wooden farmhouses of **Hälsingland** in Sweden, built in the 19th century by wealthy farmers who elaborately decorated them in styles including Baroque and Rococo. With painted murals, wallpaper, chandeliers and other finishings, they are, like all the others mentioned, examples of how an individual's house can be so special and so internationally significant that it is included on the same list as the Palace of Versailles (*see* p. 2).

The tower-houses of Shibam in Yemen are made from sun-dried bricks **Inset** Apartment blocks called diaolou in Kaiping in China are a fusion of styles

# At the movies

It may be the Hollywood celebrities who get top billing on a movie, but often it's the location that's the real star. Film-makers know the importance of a dramatic background, and that's something a lot of UNESCO World Heritage Sites offer. It's no surprise they are often featured in blockbuster movies – and have even stolen the scene in some. (Remember the Statue of Liberty at the end of *Planet of the Apes*?)

The natural sites on the World Heritage List loom large, with the deserts of Wadi Rum in Jordan (*see* p. 50) used to portray the surface of other planets, while the dramatic scenery of several of New Zealand's national parks (*see* p. 42) recreated the Middle-earth of *Lord of the Rings*. Cities feature prominently, with Bruges in Belgium (*see* p. 40) having a whole movie named after it, and ancient sites like Tikal in Guatemala (*see* p. 34) and Ait-Ben-Haddou in Morocco (*see* p. 30) are used for their distinctive aesthetics to become as easily historical as imaginary. Often these sites feel like a character in their own right, with as much of a narrative as any of the actors.

In some cases, the World Heritage Sites used in films have made such an impact on popular culture that they've inspired thousands of tourists to visit each day. While that brings some economic benefits, it also places extra pressure on sites that already needed protection.

# Angkor

## *Cambodia* (Inscribed 1992)

The moss-covered walls of Ta Phrom temple are crumbling slightly, yet they've survived remarkably well considering the site was abandoned about 600 years ago. But the walls have not been able to fight off the surrounding jungle, which has slowly entangled itself with the temple over the centuries, roots slinking across bricks like snakes, the aptly-named strangler figs enveloping whole corners of courtyards. It was here that Angelina Jolie's character, Lara Croft, went in search of a mystical item in the movie *Lara Croft: Tomb Raider* (2001), and the images of the overgrown temple in the Hollywood blockbuster took Angkor to the world.

Ta Phrom is just one of dozens of temples across Angkor, the magnificent city that the Khmer Empire built between the 9th and 15th centuries. Over an area of 400 square kilometres (154 square miles), they built successive capitals for each ruler, with majestic complexes used for administration and worship. The city area was larger than modern Paris and constructed of more stone than all of Ancient Egypt's monuments combined. At its peak, the Khmer Empire ruled much of Southeast Asia and parts of southern China until it was conquered by Ayutthaya (*see* p. 244).

The most impressive of the temples is Angkor Wat, which gives its name to the whole archaeological region. Built by Suryavarman II and still the largest religious structure in the world, its main section is sited at the end of a causeway and built on a series of terraces with a central tower representing Mount Meru (the home of the gods) flowing down to smaller towers, then to an outer wall, and on to a moat surrounding the whole complex. Different sections of the temple are connected by steep stone staircases and colonnaded passages where you might suddenly emerge from a dark corridor into the blazing Cambodian sun.

The sun rises over Angkor Wat, and it's a popular place for travellers to see the dawn of a day. From early light, hot-air balloons rise into the sky, and eager visitors rush to be the first to climb to the top for views across the orange glow of the jungle. As the hours go by, thousands of tourists spill into the archaeological park and zip around to different sites on bikes, motorcycles, tuk-tuks, cars, and buses.

Angkor Thom, just a kilometre from Angkor Wat, is the last capital of the Khmer Empire, a mini-city built from the 12th century with a number of significant temples. The most iconic is the Bayon, which has enormous faces carved into the towers of the temples, 216 of them staring out serenely with a slight smile, an eternal happiness across their expressions. On the walls of the terraces are long intricate bas-reliefs telling the dramatic and everyday history of the empire.

Although parts of *Tomb Raider* were filmed at more monuments across Angkor than just Ta Phrom, most of them had to be digitally-altered to appear as more mysterious. However, if you're prepared to spend your days here exploring further out, away from the popular sites, you may feel a little bit like Lara Croft and find some 'lost' temples of your own.

**01.** Ta Prohm temple and the tree growing amongst the ruins made famous by *Lara Croft: Tomb Raider* **02.** The Baphuon temple within Angkor Thom, the last capital of the Khmer Empire **03.** On the walls of many of the temples are intricate bas-reliefs depicting scenes from Khmer history

# Ait-Ben-Haddou

## *Morocco* (Inscribed 1987)

Even if they had tried, moviemakers could not have created a better set than Ait-Ben-Haddou. This walled community of earthen buildings, hugging the side of a hill to collectively resemble a fortress, has been used in dozens of films, representing lands from Tibet to Egypt, in movies as diverse as *The Man Who Would Be King* (1975), *The Jewel of the Nile* (1985), and *Kundun* (1997).

The fortified village, known as a ksar, has been here since the 11th century, but the oldest buildings you'll find today are from about 300 years ago. They need constant maintenance, though, because the main walls are built with only compressed mud mixed with straw. Look closely and you'll see pebbles and bits of hay protruding from a house. But the buildings served their purpose because Ait-Ben-Haddou was on the trading route between Sudan and Marrakesh (*see* p. 56) that flourished until the 17th century, and the occupants had to strike a balance between being open for business and having strong defences.

01

The first line of defence is a tall clay wall, rising from ground level with corner towers and a central gate. It's this imagery that's proved popular for many movies and television shows, notably as the slaving city of Yunkai in *Game of Thrones* (Season 3, 2013). Once through the gate, the next defence measure is the maze of narrow pathways that unexpectedly become staircases or dead ends, designed to slow invaders while the occupants escaped to a fortress at the top. It seems the labyrinth also works on tourists, as I got lost and walked past a man selling shoes three times – which he took as my attempt at haggling.

Many of the houses in Ait-Ben-Haddou are used these days as shops, but they still have their original exteriors, some modest and others like small castles with turrets. On some walls are geometric decorations created with carved niches or mud bricks. If you can find your way, you will also come across communal buildings like a mosque and a caravanserai (inn for

travellers). But they are not as busy as they once were – only a few of the homeowners live here these days, a nearby village with modern conveniences offers more comfort.

Who can blame them? The noise of Hollywood constantly arriving to film on your doorstep might get irritating after a while, especially when the village became particularly popular with top directors, with Ridley Scott making two movies here, *Gladiator* (2000) and *Kingdom of Heaven* (2005), and Oliver Stone filming some of his epic *Alexander* (2004). When the first residents built the ksar here on the trading route, they wouldn't have expected their most profitable business to be show business.

**01.** A tall clay wall with a defensive gate is a popular backdrop for movies and television shows **02.** A turret rises above a house and offers a view across the land beneath **03.** Although most houses are privately owned, only a handful of people still live in Ait-Ben-Haddou

# Hongcun

## *China* (Inscribed 2000)

When director Ang Lee was creating the world for his Academy Award–winning film *Crouching Tiger, Hidden Dragon* (2000), he set it within the Qing dynasty but was intentionally vague about the exact time or place. 'The film is a kind of a dream of China, a China that probably never existed, except in my boyhood fantasies,' he said in the movie's production notes. He did well to choose to film some of it in Hongcun, a small village in Southern Anhui founded in 1131 CE with periods of prosperity in the 16th and 19th centuries that have left a landscape fitting of fantasy.

Delicate white houses with grey tiled gabled roofs are reflected in the mirror-like waterways along which they're set; green mountains form the background in the distance; and, often, a slight fog hovers in the air between them. From an arched bridge over the water, you can see lily pads near the shore, and the long leaves of trees drooping down to try to touch them. Hongcun is peaceful enough to appear in *Crouching Tiger, Hidden Dragon* as a destination for meditation, but also dynamic enough for the martial artists to dance across its water.

Coincidentally, Hongcun (along with the nearby village of Xidi) was designated as a World Heritage Site just days before the movie's theatrical release. It was determined to be one of the best examples of a traditional Chinese village, where inhabitants are linked by blood ties, agriculture is the main industry, and the urban design is in harmony with the natural environment. The houses are simple but elegant, with graceful ornamentation. The streets follow the open watercourse running through the whole village, past every residence, that forms two large ponds, practical and picturesque.

Just a few kilometres away is the Mukeng Bamboo Forest, the setting for one of the movie's most memorable scenes, as two fighters weightlessly glide and leap across the canopy. The natural environment is in constant

interplay with the narrative, and the most striking landmark in the region is Huangshan Mountain, also a World Heritage Site, and just 20 kilometres (12 miles) from Hongcun. The granite peaks soar up through a perpetual sea of clouds, gnarled trees finding life in the stones and emerging from cracks on the cliffs. It has long been an inspiration for artists, and its landscape is still a dream for a visionary like Ang Lee.

# Coincidentally, Hongcun was designated as a World Heritage Site just days before the movie's theatrical release.

**01.** The traditional houses with gabled roofs are reflected in the water **02.** Fog often hangs in the air around Hongcun **03.** Pine trees growing out of the rock on Huangshan Mountain

## 02

**01.** Temple I, also known as the Temple of the Great Jaguar, is 55 metres (180 feet) high **02.** The spot from where a scene from *Star Wars: A New Hope* was filmed to depict Yavin 4 **03.** The tallest temples and pyramids of Tikal poke through the top of the jungle **04.** Tikal was once a great metropolis and one of the largest cities of the Mayan Empire

# Tikal

### *Guatemala* (Inscribed 1979)

Deep in the Guatemalan jungle, the tall trees compete for dominance with the ancient stone temples built by the Maya. The city of Tikal was once a marvellous metropolis, founded in the 6th century BCE as the capital of a state that controlled much of the region for hundreds of years. It would have had tens of thousands of citizens (estimates are as high as 90,000) until it was abandoned in the 10th century CE, probably because deforestation had led to drought and unsustainable farming land.

The Maya left, their constructions remained, and nature began to move back in. It wasn't until the 1950s that any serious excavation work began on the site and the jungle was pulled back to again reveal this superb city. Now that the layout is clearer, you can see that Tikal's focal point is the ceremonial square known as the Great Plaza. On its eastern side is Temple I, also called the Temple of the Great Jaguar, 55 metres high (180 feet) with nine stepped layers and a central staircase running up the middle of its façade. You get an excellent view of it by climbing to the viewing platform of Temple II, or the Temple of the Masks, on the opposite side of the plaza.

But follow the dirt paths through the thick jungle and the intrepid traveller can discover dozens of other structures, like ancient stone skyscrapers reaching up into the blue. The biggest at Tikal is the 67-metre-high (220-foot) Temple VI, which is the second-tallest pre-Colombian building in North or South America. It is also from where the makers of the original *Star Wars* movie, *Star Wars: A New Hope* (1977) filmed a scene. Climbing up the steep coarse steps to the top, looking out, you see a carpet of canopy with the tops of several stone temples poking out above the leaves. This is how the scene appears as a rebel watches the Millennium Falcon landing on Yavin 4 as they prepare to attack the Death Star.

The *Star Wars* franchise has used a lot of World Heritage Sites for filming over the years. Italy's Caserta Palace stood in as Queen Amidala's royal home; Redwood National Park in the USA was used as the home of the Ewoks on the planet Endor; and the early monastic complex on a hard-to-reach island of Sceilg Mhichíl (Skellig Michael) in Ireland featured prominently in the latest series as the home of Luke Skywalker. These other planets look a lot like ours ... just as fantastical.

The city of Tikal was once a marvellous metropolis, founded in the 6th century BCE as the capital of a state that controlled much of the region for hundreds of years.

# From real to reel

While some places appear in movies as themselves, and some are used to represent imaginary or unidentified locations, film-makers often have trouble getting access to famous landmarks or are not too concerned with the accuracy of these matters – which is why quite a lot of World Heritage Sites are actually used to portray other sites with World Heritage status.

Moviemakers often have to look for alternative locations. The Maltese capital of **Valletta**, for instance, its historic centre UNESCO-protected, was used to represent Ancient Rome in *Gladiator* (2000) and as Old Jerusalem in *Kingdom of Heaven* (2005). In *The Passion of the Christ* (2004), director Mel Gibson chose to shoot scenes in the Italian city of **Matera** to depict the time of Jesus.

The Vatican is another World Heritage Site that can be difficult to get permission to make a movie in. So, many of the scenes in the thriller *Angels and Demons* (2009) were actually filmed at the **Royal Palace of Caserta**, the enormous residence built by the Bourbon kings in the 18th century near the Italian city of Naples.

In Germany, the **Würzburg Residence** is an interesting site because this opulent palace, designed as a home for the region's prince-bishops in the 18th century, was completely rebuilt over 42 years after it was extensively damaged in World War II. It was used in *The Three Musketeers* (2011) to film scenes purportedly in the Louvre in Paris. Meanwhile, the gardens and the castle at **Kroměříž** in the Czech Republic were the shooting location for *Amadeus* (1984) to portray Belvedere Palace in the Austrian capital of Vienna.

And in the film *Onegin* (1999), **Blenheim Palace** in the UK (*see* p. 12) was used to film scenes that depicted the Winter Palace in St Petersburg, Russia. The first Western film to be completely shot in post-Soviet Russia, *Anna Karenina* (1997) does a marvellous job at showcasing the beauty of **St Petersburg** by shooting on location.

Even if a World Heritage Site is not the focus of a movie, seeing the real deal on the big screen gives it life. We feel the heart of the ancient Japanese cities of **Kyoto** and **Nara** in Akira Kurosawa's classic *Rashomon* (1950). In *Sissi* (1955), Vienna's **Schönbrunn Palace** shows why the grand Habsburg residence is celebrated as one of Austria's most impressive landmarks. The 12th-century **Abbey of Fontenay** in France creates the perfect romantic backdrop for Gérard Depardieu and Anne Brochet in *Cyrano de Bergerac* (1990).

Royal Palace of Caserta, Italy **Inset** Würzburg Residence, Germany

# Swiss Alps

## *Switzerland* (Inscribed 2001)

The Jungfrau-Aletsch region in the Swiss Alps has long been an inspiration for storytellers, from the German poet Goethe penning his famous work *Gesang der Geister über den Wassern* (*The Song of the Spirits over the Waters*) in 1779 after seeing Staubbach Falls, to British writer Arthur Conan Doyle setting an epic fight between Sherlock Holmes and Moriarty at Reichenbach Falls in *The Final Problem* (1893). In more recent decades, films have been able to showcase even more of the beauty of this dramatic landscape.

The white mountains of Switzerland have appeared several times in the James Bond movies, with so many downhill ski scenes that I often have trouble remembering which one they're from. It's hard to forget the most famous alpine chase, though, which appears in *On Her Majesty's Secret Service* (1969), in which the villain, Ernst Stavro Blofeld, has a lair disguised as an allergy clinic at the top of a mountain.

Filming of this high-altitude headquarters took place at the top of Schilthorn Mountain in the Swiss Alps, which now has a 007 Walk of Fame around it, including a plaque for George Lazenby who played James Bond in the movie. Some of the ski chase scenes were filmed with stunt actors and winter Olympians on the

01

mountain's slopes. And while Schilthorn itself is not officially part of the Swiss Alps World Heritage Site, it provides visitors with the best view of it, which features in the background of the scenes.

The UNESCO-protected area covers two main mountains – Jungfrau and Bietschhorn – which are both about 4000 metres high (13,123 feet), as well as the Aletsch Glacier, the largest, longest, and deepest in Europe. The colossal peaks, like hulking bodyguards, are covered in gorgeous white snow, glistening in the sun and brooding amongst the clouds. Together with the glacier, the landscape has a rich diversity of ecosystems, caused partly by the slow retreat of the ice flow.

Although the mountains were once purely the domain of climbers and intrepid skiers, the Jungfrau railway opened in 1912 with a 3454-metre-high (2-mile) station, making it easy for tourists to visit. But this Jungfrau-Aletsch region was chosen to represent the Alps as a World Heritage Site particularly because of the classic 25-kilometre-long (15.5-mile) vista it offers. It's best seen from Schilthorn Mountain and, conveniently, Blofeld's lair is now a comfortable restaurant – no ski chases required!

02

**01.** The dramatic landscapes of the Swiss Alps are best seen from high-altitude viewing platforms **02.** One of the reasons the Jungfrau-Aletsch region is a World Heritage Site is for the diverse ecosystems **03.** The snow-capped mountains of the Swiss Alps have inspired artists and storytellers for centuries

01

# Bruges

### *Belgium* (Inscribed 2000)

Bruges is probably the most elegant city in Belgium, where the Middle Ages are colourful, and beer and chocolate are as much about heritage as taste. Houses painted a palette of pastels, each four storeys high, front directly onto quiet canals. In the historic centre, Gothic brick monuments rise up from the streets, towers piercing the sky. From grand chateau-like buildings, flags fly high and proud, centuries of history watching them flap in the wind. And, although the original 12th-century outer walls that defined the medieval city have gone, the original layout remains, as do the four gates that mark its limits.

Full of tourists, Bruges is the perfect place for a story about two international hitmen who have to hide somewhere, which presumably is one of the reasons it was chosen as the setting (and filming location) for the movie *In Bruges* (2008). But the two assassins-in-hiding approach the city differently, and it becomes a character of its own in some ways, beguiling Ken (Brendan Gleeson) and irritating Ray (Colin Farrell). When Ken suggests they climb the 366 stairs to the top of the belfry to see the view, Ray scoffs. 'The view of what? The view of down here? I can see that from down here!'

The belfry is significant because it's also part of another World Heritage Site, a collection of 56 belfries in Belgium and France. These towers, normally attached to town halls, were symbols that a city was controlled by a council, not by a lord or a church. In Bruges,

# In the historic centre, Gothic brick monuments rise up from the streets, towers piercing the sky.

it soars above the main market square ... and Ray is actually right that the view of it is best from the ground. There are colourful and ornate buildings on every side of the square, including the large Provinciaal Hof (Province Court), built in 1887 in the Neo-gothic style, and old guild houses converted into shops and restaurants. Markets have been held here weekly since 985 CE.

The tagline of *In Bruges* is 'Shoot first. Sightsee later.' But, of course, most tourists come to sightsee first and shoot (with their camera) as they go along. These days, there are tours taking visitors through Bruges using the movie as inspiration, focusing on the sights highlighted by Ken and Ray's story. However, it's not really necessary, as you will see all of them regardless. The tight city centre may not have an obvious street pattern, but it will eventually lead you to all its killer spots.

**01.** The historic centre of Bruges has retained much of its medieval architecture and urban layout **02.** The spire of the Church of Our Lady rises up beyond one of the city's canals **03.** A statue on a bridge of St John of Nepomuk, a protector against floods

# Tongariro National Park

## *New Zealand* (Inscribed 1990)

It's in J.R.R. Tolkien's book, *The Fellowship of the Ring*, that Bilbo Baggins writes a poem with the memorable line, 'Not all those who wander are lost'. It's become somewhat of a mantra in recent years for travellers exploring the world on long journeys, some of whom may eventually, fittingly, find themselves at New Zealand's Tongariro National Park.

It was here that some of the most important scenes of the movie trilogy of Tolkien's epic *Lord of the Rings* (2001–03) journey were filmed. Director Peter Jackson, a New Zealand local, didn't have to travel far to find the epic background to represent Mordor, the fiery and desolate realm of the evil Sauron. Tongariro National Park is centred on three active volcanoes, perfect for creating the images of Mount Doom, with their mercurial activity also carving the surrounding land with steaming craters, blistered slopes, and emerald mountain lakes.

01

**01.** The volcanic landscape of Tongariro National Park was a perfect fit to represent Mordor in *Lord of the Rings* **02.** The Tongariro Alpine Crossing is 19 kilometres (12 miles) long and a popular day hike **03.** The emerald colour of the lakes is partly created by dissolved minerals from volcanic activity

The first line of Bilbo's poem declares, with a nod to Shakespeare, 'All that is gold does not glitter,' and it has never been more true than at Tongariro National Park. Despite the harsh aesthetics of the park, it has a rich cultural history and is covered in sites sacred to the Indigenous Māori, particularly the mountaintops. After lobbying from New Zealand, UNESCO changed the criteria for adding World Heritage Sites to include spiritual areas where there is nothing tangible made by humans, and Tongariro was the first of these to be inscribed.

Visitors to Tongariro National Park focus on skiing in winter and hiking in summer, although there are plenty of other ways to see the mountains, the waterfalls, the glaciated valleys, and other attractions. The 19 kilometre (11.8 mile) Tongariro Alpine Crossing through the park is one of the most popular day hikes in the country.

While Peter Jackson used the North Island to recreate Mordor, he also used landscapes on the South Island to represent other parts of Tolkien's Middle-earth. Many of them are found within the Te Wāhipounamu World Heritage Site, extending for about 450 kilometres (280 miles) up the western coast. Snowdon Forest portrayed Fangorn Forest, Lake Manapouri was part of Rivendell, and Kelper Mire was the Dead Marshes, just to name a few.

The New Zealand Government has used the connection in much of its tourism advertising, and has produced resources listing all of the filming locations, proving popular with fans of Tolkien keen on wandering without getting lost.

# Namib Sand Sea

*Namibia* (Inscribed 2013)

The Namib Sand Sea is considered to be the oldest desert in the world, having formed about 55 million years ago. Within the incredible rolling sand dunes, one small pocket stands out for its eerie beauty. A bleached white clay pan sits nestled amongst orange mountains of sand, and rising from it are blackened twisted trees, dead for more than 700 years but with a more powerful presence than ever. There was once water here but when it dried and the trees died the ground become clay, holding them in place, and the dry air stopped their decomposition.

It was here at Deadvlei, as the clay pan is called, that the opening scene of the science-fiction movie *The Cell* (2000) was filmed. It's a warped dream sequence that seems to fit the location, which could be from another world, or from your imagination. The scene also features the nearby Dune 45, an 85-metre-high (279-foot) sand dune that is the star attraction of the Sossusvlei region. In the film, a white-clad Jennifer Lopez slowly walks across the ridge of Dune 45, the ochre swept smooth by the wind broken with just her footsteps. Visitors to Sossusvlei can trace the path themselves, because the dune has been designated as open to the public. (Climbing is prohibited on most of the others – for conservation.)

This area is one of the most popular spots for travellers to experience the rolling dunes of the great Namib Sand Sea, but it's a mere fraction of the vast sandy landscape, which stretches for about 1000 kilometres (621 miles) up the coast of the country, and more than 180 kilometres (111 miles) inland. The World Heritage Site covers more than 3 million hectares (7.4 million acres) of this, the undulating hills of orange constantly shifting in the wind.

The Namib Desert is as stark as it is immense, punctuated only by small green shrubs and the occasional acacia tree, which get moisture to survive from the fog that can appear in the early morning. This powerful landscape was put to dramatic effect when it was used in Stanley Kubrick's *2001: A Space Odyssey* (1968) as the background for the opening Dawn of Man sequence.

More recently, the desert was used to film the Academy Award–winning *Mad Max: Fury Road* (2015), the bright and vivid vistas substituting perfectly for the post-apocalyptic world that was created in the movie after the collapse of civilisation from dwindling resources. Ironically, perhaps, it is this sort of future that the world is trying to prevent by protecting these natural wonders now.

**01.** The trees at Deadvlei died more than 700 years ago and have been preserved in the clay pan **02.** The orange dunes of the Namib Sand Sea stretch for about 1000 kilometres (600 miles) up the coast

Climbing to the top of the
85-metre-high (280-foot)
Dune 45 at Sossusvlei

# The curse of a cameo

Many World Heritage Sites and local economies have benefited from increased tourism after being featured in television shows or movies, but tourism can of course quickly become overtourism.

When **Dubrovnik** became the coastal setting for King's Landing in the hit television series *Game of Thrones* (2011–19), the medieval centre was often used to film scenes of political backstabbing or outright conflict. But as swords clashed in the streets, the Croatian city discovered that the whole experience, like the metaphorical double-edged sword, cut both ways. Dubrovnik's new-found fame would bring hordes of tourists, whose numbers would threaten the site's heritage.

**Tongariro National Park** and **Te Wāhipounamu** (*see* p. 42) in New Zealand still get lots of visitors looking for the lands of Middle-earth, years after the filming of the *Lord of the Rings* trilogy. But those vast natural areas can, with careful management, avoid many of the worst effects of overtourism by spreading visitors out across the parks.

The rocky island of **Sceilg Mhichíl** (Skellig Michael) in Ireland, featured in the recent movies *Star Wars: The Force Awakens* (2015) and *Star Wars: The Last Jedi* (2017), saw a 30 per cent increase in visitor numbers after their release. But it's threatening the remains of the 6th-century monastery and the bird population on the site, leading authorities to put a cap on daily numbers and not allow the visitor season to extend outside summer months.

The Austrian town of **Hallstatt**, a picturesque lakeside community, has been popular with international tourists since it was given World Heritage Site status in 1997, but numbers grew even more after its fairytale appearance was the inspiration for Arendelle, the setting of Disney's *Frozen* (2013). The crowds have angered local residents, but there's hope a new system to cap the number of bus arrivals will alleviate the problem somewhat.

Of course, there are lots of World Heritage Sites facing the pressures of overtourism even without appearing in a particular movie – think **Venice** (*see* p. 74), **Machu Picchu** (*see* p. 228), the **Great Wall of China** (*see* p. 204), and **Yellowstone National Park**. Local authorities are trying different methods to manage the problems, including issuing limited daily permits, banning cruise ships (in Venice), raising entrance fees, discouraging daytrippers, and promoting less-visited parts of the sites.

At the **Grotte Chauvet**, a cave in the Dordogne region of France, heritage managers are so concerned about damage to the prehistoric art that not a single visitor is allowed – so they built a copy exactly the same as the original nearby. It certainly solves the conservation problem, but let's hope that's not going to be the solution for every World Heritage Site.

Dubrovnik, Croatia **Inset** Sceilg Mhichíl, Ireland

# Wadi Rum

*Jordan* (Inscribed 2011)

Astride his well-dressed camel, white robes flowing around him, Peter O'Toole marches across the desert in the Oscar-winning *Lawrence of Arabia* (1962). Of course, O'Toole's depiction of the real-life British military officer T.E. Lawrence is the focus of the film, but it's the sweeping shots of Wadi Rum in the Jordanian desert that frequently steal the scene. These were the lands the actual T.E. Lawrence rode across during World War I, although the details in the dramatic retelling are quite different to the real version. Regardless, it's fitting that much of the movie was shot here – a film set sculpted by nature for millions of years, a vast sandy stage with fantastic shapes rising from the desert, where every angle looks like a new world.

Wadi Rum is about 75,000 hectares (185,000 acres) in size – roughly the same size as Singapore – but, when you visit, it appears endless. The rock formations create a natural maze of narrow gorges, sweeping arches, and steep cliffs. As they catch the sun, they change from purple to orange. At some times of the day, the sand could be yellow, or pink, or even bright scarlet. Once, ancient nomads migrated through the valleys, using the shapes of the rocks for navigation, leaving petroglyphs and inscriptions up to 12,000 years old on the cliff-faces.

Wadi Rum, with its breathtaking arid landscapes, has also been used to depict other places in film. Most notably, it was the surface of Mars in *The Martian* (2015), and was also another planet in the science-fiction movie *Prometheus* (2012), and featured in two of the *Star Wars* franchise – *Star Wars: The Rise of Skywalker* (2019) and *Rogue One: A Star Wars Story* (2016). More recently, Wadi Rum represented the deserts of Arabia again, this time in the live-action remake of Disney's *Aladdin* (2019).

**01.** The Al Kharza rock arch is one of the most impressive landmarks within Wadi Rum **02.** Millions of years of erosion have sculpted the shapes of the rocks across the desert **03.** During the day the colours of Wadi Rum change with the arc of the sun

03

# Kakadu National Park

## *Australia* (Inscribed 1981)

Mick Dundee, the original crocodile hunter, was baldly coarse and bold, of course, but in his natural confidence and colourful demeanour, he was the personification of the outback landscape that he resided in. *Crocodile Dundee* (1986) introduced the scenery of northern Australia to much of the world, with its red ochre sand, towering rock escarpments, and pockets of pristine waterways. Just like Mick Dundee told a mugger in New York, 'THAT's a knife!', the movie told an international audience, 'THAT's Australia!'.

The moviemakers spent about six weeks filming the outback scenes in Kakadu National Park, Australia's largest national park, a vast area of natural beauty and cultural significance near Darwin. Kakadu has been inhabited for more than 50,000 years by the Bininj/Mungguy people. It was one of the main reasons the national park became a World Heritage Site, particularly for the many rock art sites that tell the stories of human civilisation from millennia. You can see some of the best art at Ubirr, as part of the exploration of Kakadu National Park, where you'll need days, not hours, for a visit.

01

**01.** The Wet season brings Kakadu National Park to life
**02.** Visitors to Kakadu need to be very careful about where they choose to go swimming! **03.** The view over Arnhem Plateau from the top of Jim Jim Falls

Kakadu has a range of habitats, from the orange escarpments that stretch for kilometres, through rock gorges, to scattered forest and lowlands with termite mounds as tall as trees. The region experiences two seasons – the Wet and the Dry – and the Wet shows why the park is often more tropical than outback, with rains turning valleys into rivers, and torrential waterfalls dropping from the cliffs.

In one scene from *Crocodile Dundee*, Mick tries to explain the Bininj/Mungguy people's connection to the environment. 'They belong to it. It's like their mother.' It's simplistic and, like most of the Indigenous representation in the movie, now seems anachronistic. But it was at least a nod to the long and deep heritage found in Kakadu.

# The many rock art sites ... tell the stories of human civilisation from millennia.

# 03

# A tale of
# twelve cities

Is there anything more magical as a traveller than discovering a new city? You don't have to prefer the urban environment over the natural one to appreciate the wonder of wandering the streets, past magnificent monuments on one block and the ornate homes of residents on the next, a row of fragrant restaurants on one side of the road and hectic markets on the other.

Cities tell stories. The ruins of Aztec temples in Mexico City (*see* p. 58) tell ancient stories of civilisations, and the concrete reconstruction of Le Havre (*see* p. 66) after World War II tell modern ones of resilience. The food of George Town (*see* p. 60) talks of immigration, while the souks (bazaars) of Marrakesh (*see* p. 56) walk through imagination. Forts in Havana (*see* p. 80), pink sandstone in Jaipur (*see* p. 68), Art Deco in Asmara (*see* p. 76) – where you travel to reveals details of where a city has come from, including modern planned cities that appear to have come from nowhere!

While there are dozens of cities on the UNESCO World Heritage List, all included for their unique heritage and culture, the twelve in this chapter offer the traveller immersive and memorable experiences – and show why the tricky task of protecting evolving urban environments is so important.

# Marrakesh

## *Morocco* (Inscribed 1985)

Within minutes of arriving in Marrakesh, I was lost. Through tiny winding streets, I pushed on with no idea, past orange juice stalls with fruits piled high, dodging donkeys pulling carts, trying to avoid making eye contact with the chickens in the cages. This maze made less sense than a picture by Escher, and I was unable to tell if I was going around in circles or whether everything just looked the same. But, once I accepted my predicament, I realised this was part of the magic and adventure of the medina (old quarter), which was founded in the 11th century when urban planning was not at the front of mind.

Regardless of where you find yourself, eventually you'll find the highlights of the historic centre of Marrakesh. The stunning 19th-century El Bahia palace, where artists spent more than a decade creating the tiled mosaic floors and shaded plant-filled courtyards; the once-opulent El Badi Palace, built in the 16th century, now just walls and ruins with space for the large central pool; and the 500-year-old Ben Youssef Madrassa, the Islamic school with colourful tiles, plasterwork with Arabic script, carved wooden balconies, and an inscription over the entrance that reads, 'You who enter my door, may your highest hopes be exceeded'. It was meant for the students but it still speaks to tourists today.

The opulent palaces and large madrassas (Islamic schools) were built here because Marrakesh was one of Morocco's four imperial cities, and you'll find this rich legacy in ancient mosques and monuments throughout the city. But it's the common people who have given Marrakesh its intoxicating atmosphere over the centuries – from the large focal-point Jemaa el-Fnaa square with its carnival of magicians, snake charmers, and food stalls, to the busy market alleys of the souks (bazaars).

01

The souks seem to stretch on endlessly (and, with my sense of direction, they easily could!). There are silk-spinners and spice sellers; carpets and crystals; dyes drying and men melting metals. Each little street has its own identity and its own unique selling point. And, with almost three thousand stalls in the souks, the only things that can compete with the sight of it are the smells and the sounds, whether it's

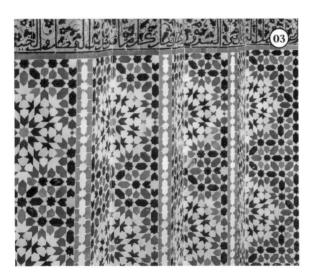

the stall owners calling to you to look at their wares, the stink of recently tanned leather, or the aromas mixing together from the piles of spices.

For centuries Marrakesh has been an influential centre in North Africa, and for centuries people have come to admire the monuments and trade in the markets. None of that has changed, although there are now also cafes, modern galleries like the Museum of African Contemporary Art Al Maaden (MACAAL), and artisans inspired by traditional local techniques. But the bustling alleys still follow the same senseless curves – and your highest hopes will still be exceeded.

**01.** The colourful souks of Marrakesh, with a huge range of wares from scarves to lanterns **02.** A beautiful internal courtyard at the 19th-century El Bahia Palace **03.** Some of the colourful tile designs on the walls of the Ben Youssef Madrassa

# Mexico City

## *Mexico* (Inscribed 1987)

At the cutting edge of fashion, art, and cuisine, Mexico City has emerged in recent years as one of North America's trendiest cities, a beacon of a new world of culture led by a young creative generation. Amongst the hip bars and fusion restaurants, there's the frenetic buzz of this giant metropolis, the country's political and economic backbone, where millions cram daily into the expansive metro while above ground the super-wealthy are chauffeur-driven through traffic jams. At its heart is the historic centre, the remarkable collection of public edifices that show how Mexico's capital got to this point.

The urban layout of the historic centre resembles a chequerboard with regular spacing of streets and plazas, the most important buildings looking onto these open public squares. The largest of the plazas is the Zócalo (officially known as Plaza de la Constitución), which is also the biggest square in North or South America. Surrounded by grand imposing buildings, it almost feels like being on the field of a stadium – an atmosphere enhanced by the constant events held in the space.

The focus of the Zócalo is the mammoth cathedral, Catedral Metropolitana on the northern side. The cathedral was built between 1573 and 1813, a confluence of styles that represent the Spanish architects and the evolution to a more independent Mexican form. But it's also a symbol of the pre-colonial heritage before the Spanish conquistadors arrived in the 1520s. Until then it was the Aztec capital, Tenochtitlan and the most important temple, known as Templo Mayor, soared to the heavens from where the cathedral now stands.

Only some excavated foundations are visible today but Tenochtitlan would once have been an impressive sight, built on islands in the centre of a lake with towers and fortresses connected by ancient canals. The Aztecs had dozens of markets within the city and grew floating gardens on the lake. The Spanish drained the water to build Mexico City, which is why the city is slowly sinking.

In some ways, it's no surprise that Mexico City is sinking – it feels heavy. There's the sheer weight of all the buildings and the streets bustling endlessly with people. But there's also the weight of history, with centuries of government and religious buildings (mainly

Catholic) built here as a European brand on the continents being claimed and converted.

But the marks of independence have gradually taken over, like in the Palacio Nacional (National Palace), first built in the 16th century, that now proudly displays enormous vibrant historic murals by Mexican artist Diego Rivera. Rivera also has works on the walls of the Palacio de Bellas Artes (Palace of Fine Arts), a marble Art Nouveau building opened in 1934 with a glimmering orange-gradient dome. Further out from the historic centre, more recent galleries like the Museo de Arte Moderno and Museo Rufino Tamayo are adding yet another layer to Mexico City.

**01.** The Palacio de Bellas Artes (Palace of Fine Arts) is one of the best examples of 20th-century architecture in the city **02.** Looking across the Zócalo to the city's cathedral, where the Aztec Templo Mayor once stood **03.** The three levels of the courtyard inside the Palacio Nacional (National Palace)

# George Town

## *Malaysia* (Inscribed 2008)

I think I would've left George Town feeling much heavier than when I arrived if it wasn't such a fascinating and dense city, encouraging me to walk almost every street – enough to work off most of what I ate. Despite being a World Heritage Site for its melting-pot of cultures, it's the cooking pots that it's just as famous for now. George Town is called the food capital of Malaysia and the sizzling sounds and smells envelope you along the streets, as much as the colourful historic houses and imposing colonial-era offices.

Both the architecture and cuisine are diverse for the same reason. George Town became the first British settlement in Southeast Asia in 1786 (with an apocryphal story that silver coins were shot from a cannon into the jungle so people would clear the land searching for them). Developed as a free port with no taxes, the city grew into a major trading and financial hub. People flocked here from countries like China, India, and Thailand to profit from the growth, and they brought their cultures and flavours with them.

**60.**   A TALE OF TWELVE CITIES

On just one street you'll find incense wafting amongst red lanterns at the Chinese Kuan Yin Temple, built in 1728; you'll also find the oldest Anglican church in Southeast Asia, St George's, with a portico of Doric columns; as well as the small Sri Mahamariamman Hindu temple decorated with sculptures of dozens of gods; and Masjid Kapitan Keling, a brick mosque with ornate green mosaics at the front and a large brown dome rising from the centre.

Near the water you'll see grand heritage landmarks built by the British: the City Hall, High Court, Fort Cornwallis; but also the six rickety jetties (one burnt down), each originally controlled by a Chinese clan, with small wooden houses on stilts above the water.

# Developed as a free port with no taxes, the city grew into a major trading and financial hub. People flocked here from countries like China, India, and Thailand.

Street vendors serve noodles, soups and snacks, and so many delectables flavoured by local spices. On the walls throughout the city are dozens of pieces of street art, many an homage to neighbourhood traditions. The diversity of immigrants that created George Town is what still defines it today.

**01.** The view of George Town, arriving by ferry from the mainland **02.** Hundreds of street food stalls across George Town have given it a reputation as a cuisine capital **03.** Works by Ernest Zacharevic are an important part of the street art scene in the city

# Damascus

## *Syria* (Inscribed 1979)

Syria is not a country for tourists right now, but let's just put aside the recent history for a moment because this region has been tested many times and has always bounced back. In its capital of Damascus, one of the oldest continuously inhabited cities in the world, you find the legacy of the unending ebb and flow of civilisations – or, as Mark Twain put it in his 1869 travelogue, *The Innocents Abroad*, 'Damascus has seen all that has ever occurred on earth, and still she lives. She has looked upon the dry bones of a thousand empires, and will see the tombs of a thousand more before she dies.'

The streets of Old Damascus are narrow and many feel even tighter from the houses that rise up from the tiny footpaths or the crowds during markets. But find the right entrance and you might slip into a calm voluminous caravanserai (inn for travellers), like the Khan As'ad Pasha, built in 1751, its large communal courtyard painted in black and white lines, nine domes creating the ceiling and an octagonal fountain in the centre.

Or you could find yourself in the Umayyad Mosque, the most important landmark of Damascus, built in the 8th century and stretching out over more than a whole city block. The enormous open-air courtyard surrounded by arcades on every side offers a form of serenity, while inside you are protected from the elements on red carpet and below chandeliers.

In the centre of Umayyad Mosque, a shrine purportedly houses the head of St John the Baptist. This is because the site was previously a church for the Christian saint; before that it was an Ancient Greek temple; and there were many other religious buildings dating

01

back to about 3000 BCE. This is the story all across Damascus, where cultures and eras meet. The Islamic call to prayer, the Adhan, is heard across the city; you might stumble on an Eastern Orthodox church or the columns of an Ancient Roman temple; neon signs announce a shisha cafe; denim jeans hang next to lanterns in shops; the souks (bazaars) are busy with market stalls, while war rumbles nearby.

In fact, the main Al-Hamidiyah Souq is still a lively focal point of the Old City, crowds pushing past each other along the 600 metre (1968 feet) street covered by a soaring vaulted iron roof. There are shawarma stalls and felafel trolleys, pastries and ice-creams, fresh juice and mint tea. And the shops along either side have everything a local shopper might need, from spices to lingerie. But that's the way it's always been in Damascus, for more than 5000 years, a cultural and commercial centre at the crossroads of the region. To quote Mark Twain again: 'Though another claims the name, old Damascus is by right the Eternal City'.

01. The layout of Damascus reflects its ancient history and the constant change of empires 02. Birds fly over the wall at the 8th-century Umayyad Mosque 03. The narrow streets of Damascus create a labyrinth through the sprawling city

**01.** The 13th-century St Nicholas Church is just one of the spires that create the skyline of Tallinn **02.** Looking out across Tallinn from part of the city's fortified walls **03.** There are 20 defensive towers still standing along the original city wall **04.** The historic centre feels medieval, but the architecture also takes inspiration from other cultures that have ruled the city over the years

# Tallinn

## *Estonia* (Inscribed 1997)

It always seems like a bit of a cliché to describe something as a fairytale, but it just seems so appropriate for Tallinn. An outer wall with conical towers where you can imagine Rapunzel throwing down her hair; a glamorous palace where Cinderella may go to a fateful ball; even a commanding castle where Sleeping Beauty could be lying in peace. Exploring the traffic-free medieval streets of the historic centre feels like turning the pages of a thousand stories that have been or could be.

If you were to approach Tallinn by sea, perhaps on a short ferry ride from Finland, you would see the skyline of the Old Town well before you arrived in port. This is by design, planned hundreds of year ago by those who wanted to project the city as a Baltic powerhouse. Most striking are the spires of the churches, particularly the 124-metre-high (406-foot) St Olaf's Church, acting like navigation aids for sailors and lost tourists alike. But the most important buildings, set higher on a central limestone hill, appear as beacons as well.

Just to the west of the historic centre, you'll find Kadriog Palace, the Baroque home built by the Russian Tsar Peter the Great in 1725 for his Empress Catherine I (even though she apparently showed little interest in it). In the Old Town of Tallinn, there's a distinctly Middle Ages feel, from cobblestoned streets to rough-brick merchant houses, and the castle-like Tallinna raekoda (town hall) from 1404. There are also refined pastel-coloured houses, a Russian Orthodox cathedral with five onion domes, and a Neoclassical palace that houses Estonia's government. Over the years, Tallinn

has changed hands between the Danes, Swedes, Germans, and Soviets, and the ensemble of architectural styles they've left takes you from guilds to gilded as you explore the walled city.

While it's the Old Town of Tallinn that makes up most of the World Heritage Site, this is a distinct contrast with surrounding parts of the city, which have become extremely modern. Tallinn is now a thriving European centre for tech start-ups and avant-garde cultural projects, with a growing population of young people moving from across the continent. The city is a beauty, yes, but hardly a sleeping one!

Exploring the traffic-free medieval streets of the historic centre feels like turning the pages of a thousand stories that have been or could be.

# Le Havre

## *France* (Inscribed 2005)

Block after block, the concrete buildings line the street like blocks upon blocks. At first glance they seem almost uniform, grey and sober, but then you notice the little splashes of colour on the balconies, the playful curves in the façades, the almost-wink in some windows. The concrete French city is not drab or Brutalist, it's beautiful in its consistency (in both senses of the word). Le Havre is, in fact, one of the most remarkable urban reconstruction projects in Europe.

Le Havre was severely bombed during World War II, and most of the city centre was destroyed or damaged beyond repair. Even before the conflict ended, the decision was made to rebuild it – but with a single blueprint. Under the direction of French architect Auguste Perret, the entire urban landscape was designed as one interconnected plan, constructed from 1945 to 1964 in a harmonious style.

One of the most striking buildings is St Joseph's Church, a square building with a 107-metre-tall (351-foot) tower that is intended to resemble a lighthouse. While the shape of the concrete exterior makes it feel slightly severe, the stained-glass windows of the tower fill the inside with a kaleidoscope of bright colours

when the sun shines through. It's reflective of the whole reconstruction of the city, where the liberal use of colours brings a sense of revitalisation to the community. The city's other most noteworthy building, l'Hôtel de Ville (town hall), stands out with its tall thick columns at the front and enormous clock tower to the side. It was intentional that the two main buildings in Le Havre would represent church and state.

If there were any fears the architecture would make Le Havre feel like a stark urban jungle, they are alleviated by the smell of the salt air that wafts up the boulevards from La Manche (the English Channel), on which the city directly sits. The concrete transitions back into sand at the main beach and the human development here seems as natural as it was designed to be.

**01.** The concrete apartment blocks are given their own character with rectangles of different sizes and colours **02.** On some of the concrete walls, murals tell the story of Le Havre's history and culture **03.** Small huts on the beach at the edge of the city are used by locals **04.** Gazing up into the colourful tower of St Joseph's Church

# Jaipur

## *India* (Inscribed 2019)

Founded in 1727, Jaipur was a planned city, designed to be a new capital of the region in north-western India. The original urban layout, although quite Western in its geometry, was heavily influenced by traditional Hindu artistic principles. So, it's fitting that the culture of Jaipur then – and now – is so entwined with the creation of artistic beauty.

Jaipur is a city of craftspeople, skilled artisans who have passed on their techniques for generations. Walk through the historic centre and you'll find specific streets and markets dedicated to crafts like painting, carving, and jewellery. Workshops open to the street and you may turn a corner and bump into someone bent over a sewing machine, a smith polishing a creation, chisels striking stone. It is a city of three million people and it's estimated there are about 175,000 who directly work in these creative industries.

Originally known in the early 18th century as the House of 36 Industries, Jaipur has a more common moniker – The Pink City. The reason for the name is obvious when you get a view across the centre and see the uniform colour on almost all the buildings. The Old City was painted pink in 1876 for a visit by the then Prince of Wales (later Edward VII, King of the UK and Emperor of India) and has stayed that way since. It's best exemplified by the stunning Hawa Mahal, a five-floor palace built from red and pink sandstone in 1799 with 953 small

windows covered in intricate latticework that give it the nickname The Palace of Breeze.

Jaipur's streets can be hectic – full of motorbikes, rickshaws, and even camels – but their planned nature also brings some structure. With continuous colonnades and businesses with uniform façades, the straight streets intersect in the centre, creating large public squares called chaupars. On a street between two of these chaupars, next to the City Palace, is Jantar Mantar, a World Heritage Site in its own right. This 18th-century astronomical observation site is a collection of 20 stone instruments, including the world's largest sundial. That the site uses mathematics but is also beautiful and carefully made is a perfect representation of Jaipur as a city.

Jaipur is a city of craftspeople, skilled artisans who have passed on their techniques for generations.

**01.** The City Palace, built from 1727, was used for political and cultural events **02.** Hawa Mahal, the palace built from red and pink sandstone **03.** The bustling streets of Jaipur were planned as a blend of Western urban layout and Hindu design styles

# Brasília

## *Brazil* (Inscribed 1987)

In a country that has the chaotic metropolis of São Paulo and the coastal vibrancy of Rio de Janeiro, Brazil's capital, Brasília, might seem a bit ... well, structured. But don't let the relative calmness of the city fool you – it's the planned layout of Brasília, with its futuristic façade and attempts at social integration that are the focus here. The architecture takes centre stage because daily life revolves around it.

Brasília was officially founded in 1960 as a new city, built from scratch on an empty plateau in the centre of Brazil, part of an effort to shift the power from the south-east of the country. Lead planner Lúcio Costa and architect Oscar Niemeyer used the opportunity of a clean slate to create what they envisioned as a modern city, combining a utopian view of society with their imagination of the future. They designed the city around a long straight east–west axis with the main administrative buildings, and a curved north–west axis, with separate residential and commercial areas, and different sectors for hotels, embassies, and banks. From above, the shape looks like a bird, a plane, or even a bow and arrow.

The Monumental Axis, 8.5 kilometres long (5.3 miles), has wide green space down the centre and six lanes of road on either side.

01

Lined with ministries, museums, and a stadium, it has plenty of empty space for future developments. At one end is the heart of the legislature, the white Congresso Nacional (National Congress) building, with a dome on one side and inverted dome on the other above the two chambers. Nearby, to one side, is the presidential office, the Palácio do Planalto (Planalto Palace), and on the other is the Supreme Federal Court, both of which have similar sleek modernist designs with columns shaped like white waves. Together the three buildings form a triangle of the three political powers of the country.

The Residential Axis is almost double the length of the Monumental Axis, and was meticulously planned with about 100 superquadras (superblocks), each a small self-contained neighbourhood with low-level apartment buildings and outdoor recreation spaces. Each was also supposed to have its own

school, church, and shopping centre – but only a handful actually do.

The futuristic urban dream turned out to be a bit of a fantasy and people still prefer to travel across town to somewhere of their choice, not just to somewhere they can see from their apartment window. The attempt to construct a society where upper and middle classes live in the same neighbourhood also only worked to a certain extent, and unexpected population growth has led to favelas (shantytowns) on the outskirts.

Still, the ambitious rethinking of a capital city plan has led to an intriguing urban centre that can be viewed equally as an architectural masterpiece and an ongoing social experiment.

**01.** Looking down the Monumental Axis towards the main legislative buildings **02.** The central zones of Brasília have statues and other monuments representing their intended uses **03.** The Museu Nacional da República, designed by Oscar Niemeyer

# Modern planned cities

Cities may begin as small organisms, but eventually they grow into complicated beasts, often much larger than their founders envisaged. The geography of a city becomes strained as the population grows, conflict can arise as inequality widens, while pollution and other environmental problems sometimes even threaten the very existence of its citizens.

Although there are many examples from history of cities that had an original plan, many of them were unable to adapt to the future. It's why the idea of 'planned cities' became so popular in the 20th century. More recently, some countries created new capital cities afresh on undeveloped land with designs that could be grown into — Washington DC (USA), Canberra (Australia), Belmopan (Belize), Abuja (Nigeria), Naypyidaw (Myanmar), to name a few — but none of them, except Brasília (*see* p. 70) are World Heritage Sites (yet).

An interesting World Heritage example, though, is Morocco's capital, **Rabat**, which has wonderful ancient mosques and a kasbah from the 12th century, but is also recognised for its huge modern city, planned and built with older sections around it. In Israel, modern principles were applied to the central **White City in Tel Aviv**, where more than 4000 buildings were constructed in an urban plan in the 1930s. The architects brought the new Bauhaus style with them from Europe, but adapted it to the local climate, with white walls to reflect the heat and small windows to keep out the sun.

There are also some fascinating towns on the World Heritage List that were planned by companies to be 'perfect' communities for their workers: **Crespi d'Adda** in Italy, **Rjukan** and **Notodden** in Norway, **La Chaux-de-Fonds** and **Le Locle** in Switzerland. The towns were designed to make the employees' lives easy and their families' lives happy ... but ultimately all in the name of profits from a more productive workforce, of course. One of the most famous examples is **Saltaire**, founded in England in 1851, where the village is set around a large textile mill and has a grid of uniform brown-brick houses interspersed with recreational spaces.

Some of these planned cities eventually had to grapple with the same issues that faced large unplanned urban centres, while others never grew big enough to feel like a real community. However, there are plenty of success stories offering a roadmap for future developments.

Rabat, Morocco **Inset** Crespi d'Adda, Italy

**01.** The Basilica di San Marco (St Mark's Basilica) on the right, with al fresco cafes in the foreground **02.** A bridge leading over a canal at the former shipyards of the Arsenale **03.** Gondoliers take tourists for a ride through a series of small canals **04.** Away from the main tourist areas, Venice can be quite peaceful

# Venice

## *Italy* (Inscribed 1987)

Along a canal, a gondola glides past a marble church and a shop covered in colourful glittering carnival masks. A busy cafe has patrons sitting al fresco sipping spritzes, while sculptures stare across a square at a pink palazzo. This could only be one city on earth (and water) – the enchanting Italian treasure of Venice.

The story of Venice begins in the 5th century CE when the Venetians moved to several islands in the lagoon to escape the raids of barbarians. Over the next 500 years, the city gradually expanded until it spread across 118 islands, and Venice became the Venetian Republic – a major maritime power in Europe and beyond. This brought wealth and the Venetians turned their city into a spectacular collection of architecture and art that made it one of the greatest capitals of the medieval and Renaissance world.

At its heart is the Grand Canal, a name that's surely an understatement because it is more than grand – it is breathtaking. Bending its way back and forth through the city, it is lined with more than a hundred palazzos and six major churches, with tall stone bridges, including the iconic Rialto Bridge, arching over the top, and a constant stream of boats along the water. At one end of the Grand Canal is Venezia Santa Lucia, the train station; at the other are the city's most famous buildings, Basilica di Santa Maria della Salute and Basilica di San Marco (St Mark's Basilica) and Palazzo Ducale (the Doge's Palace), the latter two both in the expansive Piazza San Marco (St Mark's Square).

St Mark's Square is lined by fabled cafes, bars, and shops, while the centre might be filled with market stalls, tourists, or water when the tide rises and the grates overflow. The campanile (bell tower) offers a panorama of Venice's waterways and rooftops, and St Mark's Basilica dominates the far open end of the square, with five prominent archways on the façade and five domes rising from the roof. The colourful exterior acts as a frontispiece for the inside, which glows with the warm golden mosaics covering most surfaces. The neighbouring Doge's Palace is what you might expect from the residence of the republic's ruler: opulent apartments, lavishly decorated reception rooms, and the incredible 53-metre-long (174-foot) Chamber of the Great Council, decorated with the longest canvas painting in the world, *Il Paradiso* by Tintoretto.

But Venice is more than just its recognisable landmarks, and it's in the less-visited areas that its real charm is found. An empty path along a canal where locals tie up their boats, over a bridge and past a fruit market in a square, turning a corner from a quiet alley and stumbling upon a bustling cafe. Even in these calm neighbourhoods, each building is a testament to the broader grandeur of the city, illuminated by the reflection of the sun off the water like a spotlight.

Then there are the other islands, like the famous glass-blowing Murano and lace-making Burano. With houses as colourful and creative as the wares they produce within them, it's a reminder of why this city has been an inspiration for generations of artists, writers, and travellers.

# Asmara

## *Eritrea* (Inscribed 2017)

You might be forgiven for thinking that, not only were you in southern Europe, but you were also in the 1930s. On the main street there's the Art Deco Cinema Impero theatre with crimson walls, embossed vertical lettering, and yellow bands containing spherical lights. Around the corner, a cinema from the same era has a marble façade with golden letters spelling out 'ROMA' – a clue to why this city looks like this. Because nowhere else in north-eastern Africa will you find such an incongruous modernist city.

This is Asmara, the capital of Eritrea, which was under Italian control for about 50 years from the late 1880s. In the 1930s, Benito

Mussolini wanted to create a new Roman Empire in East Africa and he chose Asmara as its nerve centre. Resources were poured into a construction boom that reflected the prevailing European style at the time – Art Deco. With little development since World War II, most of these buildings remain along the sunny streets lined with palm trees, many with signs in Italian proclaiming they were once (or still are) bars, pasticcerias, casas, or ferramentas and you'll have no trouble finding a good espresso or gelato.

Along the main wide streets of Asmara, you'll find ornate public buildings. The aforementioned Cinema Impero is one of the world's finest examples of Art Deco, but there's also the Asmara Theatre, the World Bank Building, and the Central Post Office. Yet some of the most interesting designs are found in the ordinary, like the Fiat Tagliero Building, an Art Deco petrol station resembling a plane with

For many Italian architects, Asmara was a playground in the 1930s, where they could try cutting-edge styles.

concrete wings and a windowed cockpit above the store. For many Italian architects, Asmara was a playground in the 1930s, where they could try cutting-edge styles that wouldn't have been accepted in their conservative homeland.

Before Italian rule began in 1889, there had been about 3000 people living here in a town of traditional mud huts under the control of Ethiopia (which occupied the city again from 1952). The World Heritage Site listing also includes the Indigenous neighbourhoods of Arbate Asmera and Abbashawel which evolved from the original settlement and, being unplanned, feel like a stark contrast to the city centre. Their rough dirt roads meander any way but straight, past small brick huts with corrugated-iron roofs, but Eritreans celebrate

them along with the tangible evidence from the colonial era because, together, they tell the story of the struggle for self-determination in the country which only became independent in 1993.

**01.** The design of a cafe that wouldn't have looked out of place in Italy in the 1930s **02.** The Cinema Impero is one of the most iconic Art Deco buildings in the city **03.** Art Deco was popular in Europe at the time, so the style was applied to the buildings being constructed in Asmara

# Québec City

## *Canada* (Inscribed 1985)

At one of the many excellent patisseries, I ordered an almond croissant for a little taste of Europe, but here in Québec City, you only need to look around to get that taste ... figuratively, at least. The French started building the city in 1608, and it has remained the cradle of French America for centuries, where people are generally proud of their unique francophone culture, a bridge between Europe and Canada.

Architecturally, the Vieux Québec (Old Town) is full of reminders of the city's origin: monumental 17th-century buildings like the Cathedral-Basilica of Notre-Dame, Québec Seminary, and the Ursuline Monastery – some of the oldest institutions in North America. The most important physical legacy, though, are the city's walls and ramparts, 4.6 kilometres (2.8 miles) of them circling the upper part of the Old Town, making Québec the only still-fortified American city north of Mexico.

Originally an Iroquois settlement, Stadacona, the site was soon abandoned after increased fighting with the French. Once established as a French fort, with its high vantage point on Cap Diamant and access to the ever-important St Lawrence River, it quickly became a coveted location for those looking to control the area. The city weathered many attacks by the

01

English and eventually Americans keen to take control of it.

Within the walls, wandering through the streets (many still cobblestoned) and climbing up and down staircases, the atmosphere feels Parisian, full of cafes with wicker chairs on the footpath, and boutique shops. Towering above it all is the Château Frontenac, the castle-like hotel built in 1892 by the Canadian Pacific Railway company and based on the Renaissance style in France's Loire Valley. Look closer and you'll also see the influences of the British, who took control of the city in 1763, in some of the architecture – particularly the enormous military fortress of La Citadelle, built from 1820 to defend against the Americans.

But to think of Old Québec as a mini-Paris is misguided. You'll find crêpes, but they'll be covered in maple syrup. The Hôtel du Parlement (parliament building) may be designed with the Second Empire style popular in France, but the system within it is very Westminster. And then there's poutine – the guilty pleasure of fries, cheese curds, and gravy. And even the city's name – Québec – derives from a word from the local Algonquin people, meaning strait (referring to the narrowing of the St Lawrence River, right near the city). The heritage in Québec City tells the story of everything this cosmopolitan centre has seen – from melees to soufflés – and how they've created a modern capital quite unique on this continent.

**01.** Québec City is proud of its unique heritage, blending European and North American influences **02.** The Château Frontenac is an iconic landmark in the city **03.** The cafe scene in Québec City is a direct result of the French heritage

01

# Havana

*Cuba* (Inscribed 1982)

The historic centre of Havana is a city of two layers. Palatial hotels, grandiose theatres, and colourful buildings with arcades and balconies are the legacy of one of the wealthiest colonial-era centres of the Caribbean. On top of that is the peeling paint and general disrepair that has come from an economy that's struggled since the communist revolution in 1959, a feature that Cuba describes as 'evocatively time-worn' in its official World Heritage Site listing.

The Spanish arrived in 1519 and Havana gradually turned into a bustling port for the trade between Europe and the colonies of the 'New World', becoming the third largest city of the Americas by the middle of the 18th century. The riches that sailed through Havana led to the construction of fortresses, then churches, then civic and recreational centres. What had begun as a logistical outpost turned into a chic American capital by the early 1900s, with theatres, casinos, and luxury hotels being built right up until Fidel Castro's 1959 revolution.

This rich history means that Old Havana is a beautiful collection of architectural styles, protected from modern development. Baroque, Neoclassical, Art Deco are influences from Spanish, French, British, and other Caribbean nations. Many of the best buildings are appreciated from the five main plazas, each with its own architectural character: Plaza de la Catedral with the Baroque Catedral de San

Cristóbal, Plaza Vieja with colourful buildings housing bars and restaurants, or Plaza del Cristo with an unrenovated neighbourhood atmosphere, for example.

Classic cars putter along the streets of Old Havana and, although it may seem like romantic iconography, it's because the embargo has made it almost impossible for locals to buy new vehicles. You'll spot cigars and rum in the shops, but also find small street stalls selling sweet bananas or second-hand books. What the city lacks in wi-fi, it makes up for with music and a genuine love of drinking and dancing. Away from the main sights, residences are colourful and textured, apartment blocks with wrought-iron gates leading to peaceful internal courtyards.

For a visitor, there are plenty of sights – Old Havana has about 900 historic buildings and you'll find them down any street, including the popular tree-lined promenade of El Prado. Highlights include El Capitolio (National Capitol Building) from 1929 that looks remarkably like the US Capitol, the ornate neo-Baroque Gran Teatro (Grand Theatre) next door, and the Convento de San Francisco de Asís (Convent of St Francis of Assisi) which was built in the late 16th century. Just across the water is La Cabaña, an 18th-century fort complex built by Spain and later used by Fidel Castro as a prison. It's a reminder of how the city came to be and what it came to be.

**01.** The grand buildings and boulevards of Havana are a reminder the city was once a wealthy centre **02.** El Capitolio (National Capitol Building) resembles the US Capitol **03.** The retro-looking cars in Havana still exist because it can be hard to buy new ones

# World Heritage cities in danger

One of the responsibilities that comes with a World Heritage Site listing is a requirement to protect it, something that normally falls to local or national authorities. This can be quite easy with a site like a castle or a temple, which is relatively contained and has likely been used for the same purpose for centuries – or with an area like a national park, where there's usually a predisposition to conserve the nature. When it comes to cities, though, we all know how hard it can be to stop progress in dense urban environments, and that has caused quite a few problems for World Heritage Sites.

Only two sites have ever been completely removed from the World Heritage List. One was the **Arabian Oryx Sanctuary** in Oman, which was removed in 2007 after poaching, habitat degradation, and general disregard from the government. The second site, removed in 2009, consisted of parts of the German city of **Dresden** and a stretch of the Elbe River running through it. UNESCO warned that the site would be delisted if city authorities went ahead with a modern bridge across the river, but they built it anyway, arguing that reducing traffic congestion was more important.

There are about half a dozen World Heritage cities that have been officially warned in recent years that they're in danger of losing their status because of threats to their authenticity (not including those that have been listed 'in danger' because they're in conflict zones). These include the Austrian capital of **Vienna**, because of a plan to build a new hotel complex; the English city of **Liverpool**, over the redevelopment of docklands into apartments; **Shakhrisyabz** in Uzbekistan, because of the overdevelopment of tourist infrastructure; and **Potosí** in Bolivia, because of uncontrolled mining operations nearby.

There is often a balance that needs to be struck between progress and protection. Just because a city is a World Heritage Site doesn't mean nothing can be changed or improved — that wouldn't be fair for residents, or even travellers. But UNESCO's threats to delist show there are limits, and if changes compromise a site's authenticity and the very reasons it was originally listed, its place on the World Heritage List is not guaranteed.

*There is often a balance that needs to be struck between progress and protection.*

Potosí, Bolivia **Inset** The Arabian Oryx Sanctuary, Oman

# 04

# On faith value

From the beginning of human history, religion has played a crucial role in the development of societies. Whether it's within a structured organisation, or as part of a more fluid belief system, we have always looked for deeper meanings and higher powers to explain the world we live in. The importance of faith is reflected on the UNESCO World Heritage List, with about 20 per cent of sites having a religious or spiritual connection – many of which are also covered in other chapters of this book, including the Vatican (*see* p. 114), the birthplace of Buddha at Lumbini (*see* p. 146), and the Blue Mosque in Istanbul (*see* p. 234).

Religion has inspired some of the greatest creations in our history and we see the beauty of devotion in locations like the Bagan Temple City of Myanmar (*see* p. 88), the Masjed-e Jāmé of Isfahan mosque in Iran (*see* p. 90), and the Abbey of Mont-Saint-Michel in France (*see* p. 98). These places of worship are also, in many ways, both repositories of history's greatest artistic creations and pieces of art in themselves.

There is also spirituality to be found in the formations of nature, and that's been recognised for centuries at Mount Fuji in Japan (*see* p. 100), and for tens of thousands of years at Uluru in Australia (*see* p. 94). Across the world, we have looked for connections between our environment and our deities, we have set out on pilgrimages to explore that, and we have adapted our lives to respect that.

# Old City of Jerusalem

## *Site proposed by Jordan* (Inscribed 1981)

At the crossroads of religion, the Old City of Jerusalem carries the treasures of some of the world's greatest faiths ... and the burdens of centuries of their conflicts. In just one square kilometre – such a tiny area considering all it holds – are more than 220 historic monuments that represent some of the most important events and ideals of the three largest monotheistic religions: Judaism, Christianity, and Islam.

Within the high walls that surround the dense Old City, the traffic-free alleys squeeze between steep stone buildings, up stairs, through archways, and into tunnels created by constructions overhead. The historic centre is divided into four sections – the Muslim, Christian, Armenian, and Jewish Quarters – but the architecture changes little between them, with the clothes of the residents the biggest hint to where you are.

Separate from the four quarters is the area that holds special significance for all three religions, known as the Temple Mount or al-Haram al-Sharif. According to tradition, this is where King Solomon built the First Temple for the Jews in 957 BCE, although no archaeological evidence has been found. There is evidence of the Second Temple, completed in 515 BCE and destroyed by the Romans in 70 CE, in particular the Western Wall (also known as the Kotel or Buraq Wall), a retaining wall built for the expansion of the temple by Herod the Great around 20 BCE. A small section of the wall is one of the holiest places in Judaism, where people come to pray at the limestone blocks, as close as possible to the site of the original temples.

On the Temple Mount itself is one of the most important buildings for Muslims, the Dome of the Rock. Originally built in the 7th century CE

01

but altered over the years, it has an octagonal base covered in tiles of blues and purples, with a gold-plated domed roof in the centre. It's the oldest still-standing Islamic monument and is believed to be from where the Prophet Muhammad ascended to heaven. About a hundred metres across the Temple Mount is the Al-Aqsa Mosque, one of Islam's holiest sites, which has space for about 5000 worshippers.

Although the Temple Mount is also significant for Christians as the traditional location of Abraham's sacrifice (a story that binds the three religions by appearing in all their texts), the most important Christian site in Jerusalem is the Church of the Holy Sepulchre. It was founded in the 4th century CE over the locations where Jesus is said to have been crucified and resurrected. Inside are chapels and altars in locations associated with the Stations of the Cross, but the focus is the 34-metre-high (111-foot) rotunda covered

by a 20-metre-wide (65 foot) dome with a box-like shrine in the centre that covers the Tomb of Christ.

The political status of the land has long been controversial and, because normally a World Heritage Site has to be nominated by the country where it's located, in this case an exception was allowed so Jordan could put forward the site to avoid any conflict. The aim was to protect the Old City because, ultimately, it belongs to the world. Monuments are important but, as we know, faith is about more than just the material. Jerusalem has long stood as a religious concept that transcends time and represents the perpetuity of belief.

01. The Old City of Jerusalem with the Temple Mount in the foreground 02. The Western Wall is one of the most important places in Judaism because it was part of the Second Temple 03. Built in the 7th century CE, the Dome of the Rock on the Temple Mount is one of the holiest places in Islam

# Bagan

## *Myanmar* (Inscribed 2019)

Although it was the indomitable Irrawaddy River that brought the wealth and power to build the city of Bagan a millennia ago, it's a different type of water that lends its name to its modern moniker: The Sea of Temples. Across an expanse about the size of Manhattan, where orange dust and yellow grass blend together, thousands of ancient temples rise up like islands, an archipelago of Buddhism stretched across a land steeped in tradition.

Bagan is the largest and the densest concentration of Buddhist monuments in the world. At the city's apogee between the 11th and 13th centuries, there would have been more than 10,000 temples, pagodas and monasteries here. These days, there are still more than 2200 of them, decorated inside with colourful frescoes and statues; the official World Heritage Listing covers 3595 structures, including small stupas and archaeological remains. Their earthy colours and tapered shapes make them seem almost organic, and from a distance it can sometimes be hard to distinguish between trees and temples. In the early morning or late evening, when the sun is low in the sky, there's an ethereal golden glow across the panorama.

When I visited, I borrowed a bike and pedalled along dirt tracks and over fields. The longest straight distance you can ride in the main section before hitting a boundary is about

6 kilometres (3.7 miles), so it's easy to explore. The lack of modern development amongst the ageing structures adds to the sense of exploration and discovery as you stumble across temples unexpectedly. While you can see Bagan's largest structure, the 60-metre-high (197-foot) pyramid-shaped Dhammayangyi Temple, from far away, smaller worship sites can suddenly appear from behind a grove of trees. When I walked into one of these, all I found inside was a painted stone statue of a Buddha caught in a beam of sunlight that happened to be shining through an elevated window. It was fortuitous timing that I chose ... unless the moment chose me?

The rulers of Bagan a thousand years ago controlled the maritime trade along the Irrawaddy, and they used much of the profit to build the temples as part of a Buddhist concept of merit-making – that their good deeds would earn them karmic credit for the future. For instance, King Alaung Sithu built Thatbyinnyu Temple in 1144 CE in a style that would be intentionally expensive, 66 metres high (216.5 feet), with five storeys and tapering stupas on every corner. The same concept was a factor behind renovations of the temples in the 1990s, but they were done without professional help and actually threatened the site's authenticity. Restorations in recent years, including temples like Thatbyinnyu that were damaged in a 2016 earthquake, have employed more scientific methods.

② 

**01.** A statue sits at the centre of a small temple, almost as if it's waiting for visitors **02.** Ananda Temple was built in 1105 CE and is one of the most important in the city **03.** Temples and stupas seem to stretch out across Bagan as far as the eye can see

# Masjed-e Jāmé of Isfahan

## *Iran* (Inscribed 2012)

The Masjed-e Jāmé of Isfahan (Great Mosque, also known as the Friday Mosque) was founded in 771 CE, is one of the oldest mosques in Iran and, architecturally, is one of the most significant in the world. With an iwan (rectangular hall) on each of the four sides – a new style for Islamic design – it became a prototype for impressive houses of worship from Egypt to India. Enclosed by the iwans is a courtyard that now affords visitors a bit of tranquillity from the busy streets of Isfahan, the third-largest city in Iran.

The exterior walls of the Masjed-e Jāmé jut up against the historic part of the city, a large bazaar flowing right to the main entrance.

But come inside, stand in the central open-air space, and all you will see are the gorgeous coloured tiles on archways covering each of the four sides, as though you are in a forest of mosaics. It wasn't always so peaceful, though. The Masjed-e Jāmé has only one accessible entrance for worshippers and tourists now, but previously you could enter through different doorways all around its outer walls, creating a pedestrian hub connecting the various parts of Isfahan for many centuries. You can imagine people bustling through, carrying bags of shopping, heading off to meet family, or perhaps bumping into a friend underneath an archway. It melded religion with daily life and was at the heart of the city.

01

The Masjed-e Jāmé is unique for the protracted length of time that major changes were made to its design: from the 8th century right up until the end of the 20th century. You will see the result of this as you tour through the site and realise it's made up of multiple sections, each with its own style, as additions and changes were made to the mosque for more than a thousand years.

At the core of the mosque's layout are the iwans on each side, these vaulted spaces for prayer marked by dazzling entranceways decorated with colourful turquoise and golden tiles and cusped niches. The most impressive is the southern Qibla iwan, facing Mecca, that has two minarets rising up from it and a large dome behind. Go through any of the entrances and you'll find detail upon detail – geometric carvings, intricate stucco designs, windows creating clever lighting effects, and more gorgeous tile-work. Not just a sacred site, the mosque is also effectively a museum of the greatest Islamic design styles in history.

# It melded religion with daily life and was at the heart of the city.

**01.** The entrances to two of the iwans are decorated by intricate and colourful tile-work **02.** The interior decorations were added over the centuries, creating a gallery of different styles **03.** Even though the Masjed-e Jāmé is no longer a thoroughfare, it's still a focal point of Isfahan

# Cultural Landscape of Bali

## *Indonesia* (Inscribed 2012)

Leaving the busy tourist areas of Bali by the coast and heading north into the mountainous centre of the Indonesian island, you'll drive past terraces of wet green rice paddies. Before hotels, restaurants, and bars became the main employers here, Bali was an island of agriculture, and it was from these rice paddies that the community's spirituality was cultivated.

The Balinese practise a philosophy from the 12th century called Tri Hita Karana, meaning 'three causes of goodness'. It's about respecting the harmony 1) between humans and the spiritual realm, 2) between humans and nature, and 3) between each human. And this manifests itself in the way the farming industry developed

centuries ago, and is still run through subaks: collectives of farmers who all share the same water source.

From the side of the road, I looked down at the island's largest subak, called Jatiluwih, a giant staircase of terraces, each a large rice paddy filled with water and little green shoots sprouting upwards. Between them are narrow pathways and, every so often, a small shelter or a stone shrine. The shrines are important because the locals believe the fate of their crops is intertwined with the moods of the deities – it's their land and the farmers need to ask permission to use it. To do this, all of the subak (there are 562 members at Jatiluwih) share a large temple complex in the mountains at the

01

source of their water, where ritual ceremonies are held. Smaller temples closer to the fields are shared by groups of farmers, and the postbox-shaped stone shrines within the paddies are for individuals to pay their respects to the gods.

On the slopes of Mount Batukaru, Bali's second-highest volcano, is a large Hindu temple called Pura Luhur Batukaru. When I visited, the first thing I was asked to do was splash myself from a fountain to cleanse. Throughout the complex, the idea of water is omnipresent, from the clouds hugging the volcano to the moss growing on the carved statues. Most importantly, there's the reservoir with a small shrine in the centre, where the members of the local subak come to worship before it flows down the hill and into their paddies.

Although only 20 subaks are part of the World Heritage Site, there are about 1200 of them across Bali. The spirituality is just one aspect of these collectives, with one of the main functions

to ensure the water is distributed fairly to all members so nobody is disadvantaged, even if they're furthest downstream. This is one of the three causes of goodness, part of the harmony that has kept this philosophy in place for more than 800 years.

**01.** The irrigation system of a subak is designed so all the rice paddies receive the right amount of water **02.** Pura Tirta Empul is a water temple near Ubud that is particularly popular with tourists **03.** Moss grows on a statue at the Hindu temple of Pura Luhur Batukaru

# Uluru

### *Australia* (Inscribed 1987)

It's quite hard to truly appreciate the spirituality of Uluru until you see it for yourself, a tangible beacon of the intangible, appearing almost inexplicably in the middle of the flat and dry Australian desert. In photos it often looks simply like a large red rock, but standing beneath Uluru it reveals its little details, its textures, its collage of meaningful shapes, and a whole spectrum of the earth's colours. The Traditional Owners of this region, the Anangu, have felt its significance for tens of thousands of years as part of one of the oldest religions in the world. At the foundation of Anangu life is a complex belief system called Tjukurpa, which guides the religious, moral, and cultural structure. Tjukurpa is intertwined with the

landscapes and the wildlife, explaining how they were created by ancestors, and also how they should be respected as an essential part of daily life. When you visit, you can also feel the energy of the site – a powerful invisible force that seems to radiate from deep within the rock, straight into your soul. You feel it when you follow the trail around the base, when you find patches of verdant flora near waterholes, when you see the rock art in the caves.

Uluru stands 348 metres high (1141 feet), with a base that is 9.4 kilometres around (5.8 miles). It, along with the nearby rock formations of Kata Tjuta, are just the tip, though. They actually continue for up to 6 kilometres (3.7 miles) below the ground. The rocks started to form about 550 million years ago, from sand and rock compressed by a deep sea, shifted by the movement of tectonic plates, and then shaped by erosion. The grey sandstone has

become the vivid red because traces of iron within it have rusted.

Uluṟu was once called Ayers Rock, named in 1873 after the Chief Secretary of South Australia, Henry Ayers, but is now officially called Uluṟu/Ayers Rock. One of the most important acts to honour the site's heritage came in 2019, when climbing the rock was banned, after mainstream recognition that it is offensive to Aṉangu beliefs. When the ban was first announced in 2017, the chair of the national park's board of management, Uluṟu custodian Sammy Wilson, explained in a statement why it was so important: 'Whitefellas see the land in economic terms where Aṉangu see it as Tjukurpa. If the Tjukurpa is gone so is everything ... Money is transient, it comes and goes like the wind. In Aṉangu culture, Tjukurpa is ever lasting.'

One of the most important acts to honour the site's heritage came in 2019, when climbing the rock was banned, after mainstream recognition that it is offensive to Aṉangu beliefs.

01. Uluṟu is just the tip of a much larger rock formation that continues for kilometres underground 02. A walking trail around Uluṟu is an excellent way to discover all its textures 03. Seeing Uluṟu from the air highlights how vividly the rock rises up from the flat land around it

# Natural connections

Perhaps not surprisingly, most of the religious sites on the UNESCO World Heritage List are related to the world's largest faiths, their iconic monuments and houses of worship stretching across continents. But not all religions have ornate buildings to express their belief systems. Sometimes the landscape itself forms an intrinsic part of spirituality – like for the Anangu at **Uluru** in Australia (see p. 94), and for many other Indigenous cultures around the world.

It wasn't until 1992 that UNESCO changed the criteria for World Heritage Sites to include religious and spiritual landscapes that didn't have manmade structures. It was a welcomed (but belated) recognition of Indigenous faiths and other belief systems that didn't fit into the idea that there needed to be a building in which to worship to make it a significant site.

At India's **Mount Khangchendzonga**, the third-highest mountain in the world, the Lepcha and Bhutia people have long worshipped the peak as a source of biodiversity and fertility through a concept called Mael Lyang, which says that they were created with the purest snow from the top. This has merged somewhat with Buddhism to create a unique belief system in this remote Himalayan region.

In New Zealand, the Māori tribe **Ngāti Tūwharetoa Iwi** see **Tongariro National Park** (see p. 42) as having its own life force, and as a spiritual link to their historical homeland of Hawaiki through the active and dormant volcanoes and thermal pools. There are many Māori beliefs about the park, including a story that the seven mountains around Lake Taupo were once gods and warriors.

For four of Canada's Anishinaabe First Nations — Bloodvein River, Little Grand Rapids, Pauingassi and Poplar River — their land is intertwined with their belief system. About 3 million hectares (7 million acres) of the landscape covered with lush boreal forest has been protected as a World Heritage Site with the name **Pimachiowin Aki**, which translates as 'the land that gives'. Everything the land gives to the Anishinaabe — including the flowing rivers, the moose, the tamarack trees — came from their Creator. In return, they have promised for millennia to care for it through a cultural tradition called Ji–ganawendamang Gidakiiminaan. While the elements of nature within Pimachiowin Aki hold metaphysical significance, the First Nations also have sacred and ceremonial sites where they can communicate with spirits. Some are for community healing ceremonies that involve drumming and singing, others are used for sweat lodges. Special islands and particular places in the forest are visited by young people to receive spiritual guidance through visions.

Bloodvein River, Pimachiowin Aki
**Inset** Mount Khangchendzonga

# Mont-Saint-Michel

*France* (Inscribed 1979)

The mountain that's an island. The island that's a village. The village that's a symbol of France, and one of the most beautiful religious sites in the world. Mont-Saint-Michel rises conically from the water (at high tide, at least), layers of medieval houses merging into the grand abbey and leading the eye to the glimmering point at the top, the golden statue of the Archangel Michael on the church spire.

According to legend, Saint Michael appeared to the Bishop of Avranches, Aubert, in the 8th century CE and told him to build a church in his honour – but Bishop Aubert ignored him. Saint Michael continued to ask him ... and he continued to be ignored ... until he burnt a hole in the bishop's skull with his finger and Aubert agreed to start construction.

It's hard to imagine these days that there would be resistance to building this masterpiece, but what we see today is the result of centuries of extensions. The original 8th-century sanctuary was small and it wasn't until a Romanesque

01

church was built in the 11th century that the site began to take its current form. Some ramparts were added in the 13th century, more in the 15th century, and the spire was built at the end of the 19th century.

The end result was the Abbey of Mont-Saint-Michel, the gorgeous hulking complex that dominates the top of the island, where religious devotion blends with military-style fortifications. There are dozens of rooms across several levels – from the large bright church at the top with the adjoining cloister of intricate columns and sweeping views, down the stairs to long medieval halls for dining and receptions, and then the dark damp chapels and cells deep in the mountain. These lower levels were useful when the house of God was turned into the house of the godforsaken, with the site used as a prison following the French Revolution.

When I visited, I was able to climb a hidden staircase to the abbey's roof and look out from this medieval citadel and across Mont-Saint-Michel Bay. The strong tides pull the water out to reveal a muddy floor that pilgrims have walked across for centuries, before the water rushes back in and cuts off the island from the mainland, although a causeway built in 2014 now gives 24-hour access. The causeway is particularly useful for overnight visitors who stay in the small town on the lower slope of the mountain, amongst the labyrinth of narrow streets that wind up to the abbey.

Appreciating the difficulty of building on this small rocky outcrop, let alone creating an architectural masterpiece, offers an insight into the devotion of those who took on the task (even if it required some encouragement from an archangel's burning finger).

**01.** A small statue of the Archangel Michael at the heart of Mont-Saint-Michel's church **02.** The Abbey of Mont-Saint-Michel dominates the island, with the village on the lower right-hand side **03.** For centuries, pilgrims have walked across the bay during low tide to reach Mont-Saint-Michel

# Mount Fuji

## *Japan* (Inscribed 2013)

For many travellers, Fuji-san (Mount Fuji) is the ultimate natural symbol of Japan: a snow-capped volcano with bullet trains whizzing past that can be seen from the top of Tokyo's skyscrapers on a clear day. In a country where aesthetics and order are often carefully considered, it's fitting that the shape of Japan's highest mountain (3776 metres/12,388 feet) is graceful and symmetrical, as if it was painted as decoration on a traditional shoji paper wall.

But Mount Fuji represents more than just a satisfying landscape, and for most Japanese people it's a symbol of something much deeper, something spiritual. As the path to the roof of Japan, it's been the focus of worship and pilgrimages for centuries. In traditional Japanese mythology, Mount Fuji is home to the Shinto goddess called Konohanasakuya-hime. Often portrayed as a motherly figure, she gives her children water and fertile soil, but sometimes becomes enraged and ... erupts! Rituals asking her for benevolence were often held from a distance, primarily at Fujisan Hongū Sengen Taisha Shrine, built in 806 CE about 20 kilometres (12 miles) from the summit. The Shinto traditions merged with Buddhist belief to create an ideology called Shugendo that encouraged climbers from the 12th century onwards, and in the 17th century a whole branch called Fujiko was dedicated just to worshipping the mountain with regular pilgrimages.

When I last visited Mount Fuji, I was looking for this fusion between the natural and the spiritual, and I found it in the shrines and temples scattered across the slopes. Built centuries ago for pilgrims and mountain ascetics along the traditional climbing routes, they are in harmony with their landscapes, like the Yamamiya Sengen-jinja Shrine. Here, you walk in along a path lined with stone lanterns amongst tall trees, up onto an elevated platform where you see the mountain through a clearing. There are 25 locations like this making up the World Heritage Site, including historic inns and lakes used for purification.

You can only take transportation to the 5th Station of Mount Fuji, about halfway up, and from there climbers can walk the remaining distance, which takes about six hours. But a challenge becoming more popular with visitors is the 42-kilometre (26-mile) route from the sea at Tagonoura Port to the summit. A path used by Buddhist and Shinto pilgrims for centuries, it shows the mountain's power endures with new generations.

# For most Japanese people it's a symbol of something much deeper, something spiritual.

**01.** Mount Fuji towers over the nearby town of Fujinomiya, where the Fujisan Hongū Sengen Taisha shrine is located
**02.** Climbers walk the path to the summit of Mount Fuji
**03.** The pathway leading through the forest to the Yamamiya Sengen-jinja shrine

# Camino de Santiago

## *Spain* (Inscribed 1993)

In recent times, the Camino de Santiago has grown in popularity – partly because of the movie *The Way* (2010) – and the historic pilgrimage route has become as much a rite of passage for secular travellers as for religious devotees. There are many ways to walk (or even cycle) the camino depending on where you choose to start, and these different paths are collectively called the Routes of Santiago de Compostela. All of them finish at the Santiago de Compostela Cathedral in Galicia in north-western Spain, where one of the apostles of Jesus, St James, is said to have been buried, making it one of the world's holiest Christian sites. Even if the story of St James is not front of mind for every pilgrim, the roads to be trod are usually seen as a path to something spiritual.

For days on end – usually weeks – people walk along the designated routes, past shorelines with dramatic cliffs, along dirt paths through green farmland, on cobbled roads into medieval towns, and up hills to viewpoints where the long trail stretches out ahead. Most walkers bring minimal baggage and stay in special hostel-style accommodation, called albergues

01

(pilgrim hostels), along the way. They also usually carry an official credencial (pilgrim's passport), which gives access to these hostels, each one stamping the little book as proof of the journey to get a certificate (even though you may only be trying to prove something to yourself). In medieval times, pilgrims were given a scallop shell as proof, and this is still the symbol of the camino, seen on signs across the way and often attached to walkers themselves.

Four of the main northern trails in Spain make up the World Heritage Site, including buildings such as cathedrals, churches, monasteries, and inns in 166 towns and villages. But the most popular one is the Camino Francés (French Way), which begins at the small town of Saint-Jean-Pied-de-Port on the French–Spanish border and then leads pilgrims for 769 kilometres (478 miles) to the cathedral. A separate World Heritage Site in France

covers more than 70 significant buildings along the hundreds of kilometres of pilgrimage trails across the country that lead to the start of the Camino Francés.

It was not long after the tomb said to be of St James was discovered in the 9th century that the routes first became busy, and the pilgrimage reached its peak in the Middle Ages, spreading wealth and cultural knowledge across the north of Spain. But political unrest, plague, and other social factors saw the religious journey wane in the 16th century. In the 1980s, only a few hundred people registered for the walk, but it has again captured the collective imagination and recently there have been about 350,000 pilgrims a year!

**01.** The trails of the Camino de Santiago lead through small towns and diverse environments **02.** The scallop shell is the symbol of the Camino de Santiago and is often used to mark the routes **03.** Santiago de Compostela Cathedral — the ultimate destination for pilgrims

# Walk the talk

Spirituality usually involves a journey. A metaphysical one, at least. Perhaps it's a period of self-discovery; a search for meaning or understanding; a quest with a list of challenges as long as life itself. For centuries, many religions have tried to take these experiences from the soul to the solid and give them physical form through pilgrimages – to Bodh Gaya in India, Canterbury in England, Lourdes in France, and sites across the Holy Land in the Middle East. They may often be presented as being about reaching a destination, but it's the journey that changes you (much like travel itself, I believe).

There are just three World Heritage Sites specifically of pilgrimage routes – two covering the **Camino de Santiago** trails in Spain and France (*see* p. 102), and the other through the **Kii Mountain Range** in Japan, where Buddhist and Shinto pilgrims trek amongst maple and cypress trees to temples and shrines in hilltop towns, soaking in hot springs in the evening. In Japan, there are also sacred sites on the climb up **Mount Fuji** (*see* p. 100), which many people do as a religious journey.

The Hajj to **Mecca**, Islam's most significant and one of the world's biggest pilgrimages, has been proposed as a World Heritage Site but has not been added yet. However, the nearby city of **Jeddah** in Saudi Arabia has been recognised as the gateway for Muslim pilgrims arriving by sea on their way to the holy site. In **Mauritania**, four ancient towns known as ksours (small walled settlements made from rough bricks) are listed partly because they were the gathering place for pilgrims on their way to Mecca in the Middle Ages.

In China, **Mount Taishan** has been a focus of pilgrimages for three millennia, as the holiest mountain in the country, worshipped by Buddhists, Taoists, and citizens more generally. The path to the top (1545 metres high/5068 feet) has about 6600 steps, and it takes the average climber four hours to reach the complex of temples on the peak. Along the way are hundreds of stone tablets and inscriptions. Mount Taishan now has cable cars, which can save you the long climb, but also put the idea of a pilgrimage into perspective. Everyone takes one for their own personal reasons and does it in their own way. Ultimately, the journey is inside us.

*For centuries, many religions have tried to take these experiences from the soul to the solid and give them physical form through pilgrimages.*

Mt Taishan, China **Inset** Historic City of Jeddah, Saudi Arabia

# Stonehenge

### *United Kingdom* (Inscribed 1986)

Can you imagine robed worshippers standing in the cold night with torches, the light flickering on enormous stones creating a circle of arches around them? Perhaps they would chant, perhaps one would offer a sermon, perhaps they would be silent and let the sounds of the surrounding woods envelop them? Or maybe none of this happened at all. The megaliths of Stonehenge know what really went on here thousands of years ago, but they have never shared their secrets. It's one of the reasons they are still so fascinating and one of England's most popular landmarks.

Stonehenge seems to sprout from the flat green Salisbury Plain, with 83 stones still visible, the tallest one standing 8.7 metres high (28.5 feet).

The first monument was built here about 5000 years ago and the design evolved over the centuries, with the first stones added in about 2500 BCE. When they were all in their final places, they would have created a series of concentric circles, the taller ones made from sarsen (a type of sandstone) and topped with lintels, the smaller ones from igneous bluestone and arranged individually. This central series of stone circles was tightly packed together, with a diameter of only about 30 metres (98 feet). These days, visitors need to stay behind a rope about 10 metres (33 feet) away, but the intrigue still hangs heavy in the air.

Speaking of heavy, how the stones were transported here is a mystery, although it's likely they were rolled on logs or pulled along a greased path (or perhaps they were put here by aliens, as some believe). But the bluestones came from up to 250 kilometres (155 miles) away, suggesting they had a particular significance, likely associated with the religious aspect of the site. It's believed Stonehenge was probably used as a spiritual burial site and for worshipping ancestors. Importantly, the layout is aligned with the summer solstice sunrise and winter solstice sunset, so it was probably also used as a temple to the sun.

Stonehenge is still used as a place of worship today by Pagans, Druids, and other similar religions, who are given special permission on certain days to go beyond the normal tourist ropes, into the centre of the stone circles. Whether their ceremonies are anything like the ones millennia ago, we don't know. The Neolithic culture that built Stonehenge left no written records, leaving us with many mysteries that will probably never be answered.

# The megaliths of Stonehenge know what really went on here thousands of years ago, but they have never shared their secrets.

**01.** The aerial perspective of Stonehenge shows the layout of concentric circles **02.** Standing upright and on the ground, there are 83 stones still visible **03.** Stonehenge has a special significance on the winter and summer solstices

# Sulaiman-Too Sacred Mountain

## *Kyrgyzstan* (Inscribed 2009)

The bare rocks of Sulaiman-Too rise up in the middle of Osh, an otherwise flat city that's green in summer and white in winter. It's called a mountain, even though it's only 200 metres high (656 feet), and it's called sacred, although nobody knows how it originally became that way more than 1500 years ago. One popular story is that, although Osh was on a busy part of the Silk Road, it was 50 kilometres (31 miles)

further than the first city that caravans would reach after a long tiring mountain crossing – so the local authorities declared Sulaiman-Too as sacred to encourage travellers to rest here instead. Was it basically an ancient tourism marketing campaign?

Regardless, Sulaiman-Too became known across Central Asia as a spiritual centre from

01

the 5th century CE and Silk Road travellers flocked here, particularly during medieval times. It wasn't connected with any specific religion – people believed the power of the mountain would give them luck for their journeys and cure health problems. There was a rock to slide down to fix back pain, a hole to climb through to remedy infertility, another spot for headaches, and another for long life. In some of the caves are petroglyphs from many years earlier, a sign that the mountain had significance even before the caravans arrived.

Over the past few centuries, several small mosques have also been built on the slopes, but it's still the natural formations that take the focus as you walk up the staircases and mildly inclined paths that lead you around the mountain. The exception is the tawdry Soviet-era museum built within a large cave that juts out from a cliff. The official UNESCO

listing acknowledges this when it defends the authenticity of the site, 'even given the numerous interventions over the past 50 years'. One of the strongest sacred associations that remains is the cult worship of horses, the animals that brought the Silk Road travellers here hundreds of years ago and are still critical to the culture of Kyrgyzstan.

**01.** The entrance to the museum, built into the mountain during the Soviet Era **02.** Sulaiman-Too is only 200 metres high (656 feet) **03.** A pathway leads along the side of the mountain, past some of the significant sites **04.** Looking out across the city of Osh

A copy of some of the ancient petroglyphs found painted on Sulaiman-Too Sacred Mountain hangs in the museum

# States of the arts

A great artistic masterpiece can say so much about its time. Or it can appear timeless. Art can capture a generation of history in a single work, be the defining images of a culture for centuries, or herald an evolution in society before people even realise it's happening. They say a picture tells a thousand words, and it's through artworks that we can read the story of humanity – although everyone has their own interpretation.

Some of the most important World Heritage Sites have been protected because of the art within them – from famous galleries like the Louvre in Paris (*see* p. 118), to remote and ancient rock art at Argentina's Cave of Hands (*see* p. 122). They have been sculpted to stand out like New York's Statue of Liberty (*see* p. 126), become an icon of a city like the Sydney Opera House (*see* p. 128), or are hidden away like the Dambulla Cave Temple in Sri Lanka (*see* p. 120). They each represent not just masterpieces, but movements.

In some cases, the artworks are also a celebration of the artists – names that are still globally renowned centuries later. But sometimes the artists' identities have been lost in time ... or were never known, because their work said it all.

01

# The Vatican

## *Holy See* (Inscribed 1984)

Reaching out, finger extended, the image of God almost touches the hand of Adam, giving life to the man the Bible says was the first. But it could just as easily be an image of the artist giving life to art itself, because this painting at the Vatican's Sistine Chapel is one of the world's most inspiring creations.

The fresco is officially called *The Creation of Adam* and it was painted by the famous Italian artist Michelangelo on the ceiling of the chapel, part of a much larger decoration scheme he worked on from 1508 to 1512. It's one of nine main frescoes down the centre of the ceiling depicting God's creation of Earth, the story of Adam and Eve, and the subsequent plight of humanity.

While it's Michelangelo who is normally associated with the Sistine Chapel – and it's worth noting he also painted the chapel's altar wall with the 14-metre-high (45-foot) blue fresco *The Last Judgement*, which has more than 300 figures in it – some of the most famous artists of the Renaissance also contributed their skills here. There are wall frescoes by Sandro Botticelli, Domenico Ghirlandaio, and Pietro Perugino, plus a set of large tapestries by Raphael. Standing there in the Sistine Chapel, although it's a large space, it feels so full with all the talent it contains.

If you didn't know better, you might think the Vatican is just one enormous art museum. It certainly has one of the largest and most valuable collections in the world. Your neck may strain from staring up at the Sistine Chapel's ceiling, but your feet will hurt more from walking through kilometres of the Holy See's galleries. Within St Peter's Basilica, the largest church in the world and the centre of the Catholic faith, there are scores of priceless works. The most famous is another piece by Michelangelo, a marble sculpture of Jesus on the lap of the Virgin Mary after his crucifixion, called *Pietà*. On the walls are colourful mosaics (because, unlike paintings, they won't fade), with one of the most impressive being a reproduction of Raphael's masterpiece *Transfiguration*, showing Jesus radiating with light at the top of a mountain.

The original of Raphael's artwork is not far away, in the Vatican Museums, which were founded in 1506. There are more than 70,000 items in the collection, although only about 20,000 are usually on display. They include not just the most important Christian artworks by masters like Leonardo da Vinci and Caravaggio, but artefacts from antiquity and more contemporary works by Pablo Picasso, Vincent Van Gogh, and other modern painters. Vatican City may be the smallest country, but it holds so much of the world within it.

If you didn't know better, you might think the Vatican is just one enormous art museum. It certainly has one of the largest and most valuable collections in the world.

**01.** The interior of St Peter's Basilica is covered in opulent artworks **02.** The entrance to St Peter's Basilica **03.** A bronze artwork called *Sfera con sfera* (sphere within sphere) by Italian sculptor Arnaldo Pomodoro

# Valley of the Kings

*Egypt* (Inscribed 1979)

For a civilisation that existed millennia ago, we still have such a strong fascination with the art of Ancient Egypt, with many of the world's most famed museums dedicating large galleries to their collections from the empire. But the greatest gallery of Ancient Egypt is still in situ, within the tombs of the pharaohs at the Valley of the Kings near Luxor.

On the surface, the site doesn't offer much – just pathways through the dusty, shadeless desert between mounds with half-hidden cut-outs. But through each of these entrances is a long colourful passage leading through the chambers dedicated to the life (and afterlife) of a ruler. When they were sealed for the first time, they would have been full of treasures – golden statues, ornate jewellery, ceremonial

masks, carved furniture, even boats. But grave robbers beat archaeologists to these tombs by several thousands of years. (Except, of course, that of Tutankhamun, which revealed one of the most glorious acquisitions from the ancient world.) What they couldn't steal, though, were the paintings on the walls, and these are a rich treasure trove for us today. They show scenes from the life of the pharaoh, the ruler meeting the gods, glorifications of their accomplishments, and depictions from religious texts.

Walking down the tombs, almost climbing in some steep parts, you feel like you're descending into a dark yet vibrant ancient gallery that once would have been lit only by flickering flames. The longest tomb in the Valley of the Kings,

01

belonging to Seti I, goes for 138 metres (453 feet) and has a rich blue ceiling in parts, with golden walls covered in hieroglyphs and thousands of images of people. Tutankhamun's tomb was discovered here in 1922, but in total 64 tombs have been discovered in the valley – although only 18 are ever opened to the public.

Egyptian art served a practical purpose – to give people and their stories permanence, taking them from this life into eternity. The styles of individual artists were not to be expressed, because the form was universal (and of the universe). Figures were almost always painted with heads in profile, torsos facing forward, and both legs showing. The bigger the figure, the more important they were. Colour was also used consistently – men with red skin, women lighter, gods in gold, and the underworld's deity Osiris as green or black. And even the creation of the paints across eras changed little because artists used the same recipes for the colours – for instance, mainly

oxidised iron for red, a copper mineral called malachite for blue, carbon for black, and chalk and gypsum for white.

Although you can find examples of these artworks in museums across the world, nothing can replace the experience of seeing the vibrant colours within the tombs where they were first painted … ironically, where they were never supposed to be seen again by a living soul.

---

01. Some of the wall art from within the tomb of Ramesses V and Ramesses VI, which has a great variety of decoration 02. In Egyptian art, figures were usually painted with heads to the side, torsos forward, and both legs visible 03. The entrances to the tombs give no indication of the treasures you'll find within them

# The Louvre

## *France* (Inscribed 1991)

The large glass and metal pyramid at the entrance to the world's most famous art gallery – the Louvre in Paris – is now almost as famous as the gallery itself. Designed by I.M. Pei and built in 1989 to help direct the huge crowds of visitors, the pyramid is a modern addition to a site first built in 1190 CE as a fortress to protect the city. (How apt it now protects the city's treasures.) Over the years, the Louvre was expanded many times into a luxurious residence for the Kings of France with vast halls to display their art collections but, despite its grand history as a royal palace, the most famous resident is the Italian noblewoman Lisa Gherardini. Or, as most people know her, Mona Lisa.

The *Mona Lisa* is an intriguing painting because, despite its perfection, there are many things we don't know about this image of a woman sitting, hands crossed, with a background of winding paths and icy mountains. Experts disagree slightly about who the subject is, exactly when Leonardo da Vinci painted it (although it was sometime in the early 1500s), or how it ended up in France. Even the smile of the Mona Lisa is enigmatic. Is she smiling at me or something she is thinking about? Was she smiling before I looked at her ... because there seems to be motion in her lips? (That's no accident because when Leonardo wasn't painting, he was often cutting up human bodies to study how the muscles and skin of faces worked.)

Of course, the *Mona Lisa* is just one of about 380,000 items that the Louvre has in its collection, with about 35,000 on display at any moment, ranging from ancient classics to modern works. It would take days to walk through its galleries and see everything, which is why some visitors focus on prominent pieces like the Ancient Greek statue *Venus de Milo*; works by acclaimed artists such as Michelangelo, Caravaggio, and Albrecht Dürer; or the most famous French painting, *Liberty Leading the People* by Eugène Delacroix, depicting the French Revolution of 1830 that

saw Charles X, the last Bourbon king of France, removed from the throne. As well as the many painting galleries, there is a huge number of sculptures, one of the world's largest collections of Ancient Egyptian art, and decorative pieces collected by the French kings and emperors.

The Louvre is just one of the landmarks that makes up the World Heritage Site in Paris that stretches along the Seine, with landmarks including Les Invalides (with its central

golden dome), the Grand Palais, and Notre Dame Cathedral (which hopefully we will one day see restored to its glory). As you stroll along the banks of the river, you are never far from world-renowned art. There's the Musée d'Orsay, the former train station that contains the world's largest collection of Impressionist masterpieces; the Musée de l'Orangerie, home to eight of Monet's large *Water Lilies* paintings; and the Art Deco Palais de Tokyo with its huge contemporary exhibition spaces.

With so much art to see in Paris, it's a bit perplexing that you still get huge crowds waiting in long lines to see the *Mona Lisa* for mere seconds. Maybe that's what she's smirking about.

**01.** Looking up through the glass pyramid at the entrance to the Louvre **02.** Leonardo da Vinci's *Mona Lisa* is the most famous painting in the museum **03.** The Louvre has an excellent collection of classical art amongst its 380,000-item collection

# Dambulla Cave Temple

## *Sri Lanka* (Inscribed 1991)

Walking up the path and staircases to the Dambulla Cave Temple feels harder than the 400 metres (1312 feet) should – and not just because of the steep sections. The Sri Lankan humidity and water bottle–grabbing monkeys also make it seem more arduous. But perhaps it's fitting that there's a degree of difficulty in the approach to such an important pilgrimage site, because it makes the calm upon arrival seem even more pronounced.

At the top of the 160-metre-high (525-foot) rock are five natural caves, quiet and cool, that were filled with dynamic statues of Buddha in the 12th century. There are 153 of them – different sizes, different poses, painted in gold or red – and they almost seem alive with their open eyes staring. Some tower over everything else and dominate a cave, while others sit together in a row, seemingly guarding the wall behind them. And the walls of the caves deserve to be guarded, just like the ceilings, because they are covered in paintings of vibrant reds and yellows that fill the space. The paintings are of geometric patterns, iconography, and scenes from Buddha's story, including leaving

01

home on his journey to Enlightenment and his first sermon.

Buddhists first started living in the caves more than 2000 years ago, not long after the religion arrived on the island, and the site gradually evolved as monastery, shrine, and then temple. It's thought the first paintings were done on the walls of Dambulla's caves in about the 8th century, but over the years they've been repainted with different stories and in different styles. Most of the ones you can see today are from the 17th and 18th centuries, although some of them are similar in style to the art found at nearby Sigiriya, a fortress built on a rock in the 5th century. Presumably the later artists of Dambulla were creating a connection to the past, honouring the heritage of the caves, which have now played a sacred role for at least two millennia.

It is still a pilgrimage destination and place of worship, so you'll need to dress modestly and take off your shoes before entering. But while guards keep an eye out for anyone misbehaving, it's really those pesky monkeys that you have to watch out for!

**01.** Vibrant paintings on the ceilings bring colour to the caves at Dambulla **02.** The temple has 153 statues of Buddha **03.** The first statues were put here in the 12th century CE **04.** A statue of a reclining Buddha in one of the main caves

# The Cave of Hands

## *Argentina* (Inscribed 1999)

It took me more than a day of rumbling across the plains of rural Patagonia (it's not all mountains and glaciers) just to reach this spot, the stone wall of a cave with dozens of handprints. Orange, yellow, and red pigments sprayed onto the rock, while hands were placed on its cold hard surface, have left the impressions in negative of fingers and palms. They're ancient hands, from 9000 years ago, when there would've been more than just me and the local ranger here. Millennia ago, whole communities of nomadic hunters would pass

through this valley and stay in the caves as they followed their prey across Argentina.

The hunters of Patagonia documented their stories in the art of the Caves of Hands. They would've sprayed the paint through a pipe made of animal bone, presumably holding it in their right hand because the shapes on the wall are of the left. Each handprint was a personal acknowledgement of their life, and each group of hands a demonstration of their community.

Around the hands they drew pictures of their daily activities. The drawings show men chasing guanaco (a llama-like animal that was the main source of food) with primitive weapons but ingenious tactics. In one tableau, a crack in the rock is used to represent a ravine that the hunters chased the animals into, making them easier to catch. There are also images of their weapons called bolas, a cord with weights on each end, that could be thrown at the legs of their prey to trip them over.

There are lizards and spiders, pregnant animals, baby animals, and even evil spirits in the drawings. The things that made up their world are all depicted on the rock.

I remember asking the ranger about some dots painted on the roof of the cave. 'They could be the stars in the sky ... or maybe the marks of a game where the children would throw painted balls into the air,' she chuckled. 'We don't really understand everything.'

The paintings and hand stencils stretch out along the rock-shelters for at least 100 metres (328 feet), with more than 800 prints on the walls. Generation after generation would have added their marks as they passed through on their hunts. You can almost picture a tribe sitting here, hunched around a fire, eating

their guanaco, turning its skin into clothes, and painting the stories of the day on the walls around them. You don't need to wish that these walls could talk – the artwork already says so much.

# Each handprint was a personal acknowledgement of their life, and each group of hands a demonstration of their community.

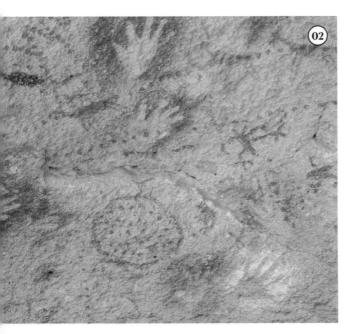

**01.** The nomads created their handprints by blowing paint through a pipe **02.** The handprints and paintings are about 9000 years old **03.** Looking out at the valley that stretches beneath the rock faces

# Rock art around the world

Long before painters stretched fabric across wooden frames, humans were using the walls of caves as their canvas to tell their stories. The Cave of Hands in Argentina (see p. 122) is just one of many World Heritage Sites that have significant collections of rock art from centuries (or millennia) ago, and they're found on every inhabited continent.

Colombia's **Chiribiquete National Park** is a fascinating site where sheer-sided sandstone plateaux rise out of thick inaccessible forest. More than 75,000 figures have been painted in rock-shelters showing hunting and dance scenes, and new paintings are still added to the walls by Indigenous groups voluntarily isolating or uncontacted by the outside world! These tribes include the Tanimucas, Cabiyaries, Matapis, Cubeos, Desanos, Huitotos, Boras, Mirañas, Yukunas, Tucanos, and Karijonas, among others.

**Writing-on-Stone Provincial Park (Áísínai'pi)** in Canada has more than 50 petroglyphs sites where the Blackfoot Confederacy (Siksikáíítsitapi) carved shapes into stone columns that have been sculpted by erosion. The engravings are up to 3000 years old, many of them interpreted as messages to the spirits.

France's **Cave of Pont d'Arc** has a collection of some of the world's oldest rock art, dated to about 30,000 years ago. What makes the thousand or so images so spectacular is the detail in the painting, including skilful shading, three-dimensional perspective, and accurate animal anatomy.

The site of **Tassili n'Ajjer** in Algeria has one of the most important collections of prehistoric cave art in the world, telling the stories of animal migrations across Africa, changes in the climate, and human evolution on the edge of the Sahara Desert from about 6000 BCE.

The rock-shelters at **Bhimbetka** have the earliest traces of life in India, with paintings on the walls from about 10,000 years ago. The images of animals and ceremonies were added to over the millennia, offering an insight into the changing culture of the people here, some of which can still be seen in the traditions of the local villages of the Gonds, Pradhans, and Korkus peoples.

In Australia, although several World Heritage Sites have examples of Indigenous art, one of the most significant places is **Murujuga**, likely to be added to the World Heritage List soon. This peninsula and islands in Western Australia have the largest concentration of rock art in the world, with more than a million carved petroglyphs by the Ngarda-Ngarli people, some up to 40,000 years old and of animals that are long extinct.

Writing-On-Stone Provincial Park (Áísínai'pi), Canada **Inset** Bhimbetka, India

# The Statue of Liberty

## *United States of America* (Inscribed 1984)

She stands silently but speaks volumes. The Statue of Liberty in New York Harbour raises her right hand to hold aloft a torch, covered in 24-carat-gold, representing progress and enlightenment. In her left hand she holds a tablet with the date of the Declaration of Independence inscribed in Roman numerals. Her crown, with seven rays, suggests the sun, the seven seas, and the seven continents. And in its entirety, this single copper sculpture, 46 metres high (151 feet), symbolises a nation.

The Statue of Liberty was given to the people of the United States of America from the people of France to commemorate the centenary of American Independence in 1776, although it wasn't dedicated until 1886. It was designed by Frédéric Auguste Bartholdi and built by Gustave Eiffel (who would go on to become more famous for his eponymous tower in Paris).

The figure is a portrayal of the Roman goddess Libertas, and Bartholdi gave much thought to the symbolism of the design. For instance, he chose to dress her in robes so she wouldn't look like the depiction in the famous Delacroix painting *Liberty Leading the People* (in the Louvre, *see* p. 118). But often it doesn't matter what an artist intended – the viewers of a work create their own meaning, and that has certainly been the case with the Statue of Liberty, which has represented different ideals to different generations of Americans.

01

## 02

The statue was originally supposed to be a symbol of democracy and freedom, the broken shackles at the woman's feet a reference to the abolition of slavery. Yet Black Americans largely dismissed the meaning of the statue because they still endured racism and discrimination. It ended up meaning more to new immigrants to the United States (14 million arrived in the country in the 40 years after the statue was erected), with the robed woman holding a torch becoming a romanticised welcome that could be seen from ships. Ultimately the Statue of Liberty came to be a personification of the whole country, leading troops into battle in war posters, or its toppling in movies denoting an alien attack or natural disaster.

Originally the sculpture was called *Liberty Enlightening the World*, and the name is apt because the evolution of its portrayal is an enlightening look at the culture of the country it represents.

**01.** The Statue of Liberty was built by Gustave Eiffel, even more famous for his tower in Paris **02.** Arrivals by boat to New York City often sail past the Statue of Liberty **03.** The tablet in the statue's hand has the date of the US Declaration of Independence

# Sydney Opera House

*Australia* (Inscribed 2007)

The sails of yachts glide across Sydney Harbour while, on the edge of the water, it's a cascade of static sails that captures the attention. The Sydney Opera House, the city's most iconic building, is made up of three sets of interlocking sails, an homage to the boats that fill the harbour. Or perhaps they more closely resemble shells, a nod to the city's popular beaches, or to the middens (mounds of waste) of shells found on the site from the feasts the Gadigal people once held here. The Gadigal people would also sing, dance, and tell stories on this spot, known as Tubowgule, so it's worth acknowledging city onto the global stage when it was opened in 1973.

Speaking of stages, there are actually six venues within the building (and the forecourt can be used as a seventh). The largest is the Concert Hall, underneath the north-western set of sails and with about 2000 seats, which is used for the main orchestra performances and, in recent years, modern gigs like Kanye West and The Cure. The second-largest space is the Joan Sutherland Theatre (known as the Opera Theatre until 2012), where operas and ballets are performed to about 1500 people. (You may notice a net over the orchestra pit, which was installed in the 1980s when a chicken walked off the stage and landed on a cellist.)

As a piece of art, the Sydney Opera House is controversial, though. The design by Danish architect Jørn Utzon was chosen in a competition because of its inspirational imagery, but during the construction phase, the architect and the state government fell out as politics, finances, and creative vision, clashed together. Utzon resigned and left Australia, and the building was finished by different architects, his original vision altered and incomplete.

But there was a reconciliation of sorts, and a decade before his death he developed a set of design guidelines that officials agreed to use for any future modifications. Perhaps the greatest tragedy is that Jørn Utzon never returned to Sydney to see his creation before he died in 2008. Although Utzon may never have laid eyes on the Sydney Opera House, more than

11 million people visit it every year to appreciate his brave visionary design that has become an icon of the city.

**01.** Looking across Circular Quay to the Sydney Opera House
**02.** The creation of the shape of the sails is considered an engineering marvel for its time **03.** A staircase inside the Sydney Opera House, leading to one of the theatres

# La Sagrada Família

**Spain** (Inscribed 1984)

The soaring spires of La Sagrada Família define the Barcelona skyline as much as the cranes that have also risen from the basilica for decades. Construction began in 1882 and it's still ongoing, such was the epic vision of its local architect, Antoni Gaudí. The eight spires that already exist (ultimately there will be 18 of them) look like they have grown up from the ground, perfectly organic in their imperfections, with outstretched roots and hanging drips. The unexpected curves and dimples make it look almost like a sandcastle, almost unrecognisable as a basilica except it still follows the basic architectural conventions of a Christian church.

One of the reasons Gaudí has become such an iconic figure is for his unique style, which evokes images of the natural world with its flow and plant-like shapes. Even standing inside in the centre of La Sagrada Família feels like you're amongst a forest, columns branching out like trees at the top, and dappled light coming through windows, as though the sun is shining between leaves. Virtually nothing is flat, it's made to feel like it wasn't made. And incorporated into it all are passages from the Bible or symbols of the life of Jesus, a result of Gaudí's belief that the best way to commune with God was to abide in nature.

01

While his work at the basilica continues, there are six other completed places in Barcelona that make up the World Heritage Site dedicated to the architect. A popular one is Park Güell, where nature blends in with Gaudí's design of winding paths, colourful mosaics, bird nests in walls, and serpentine-shaped seating.

In the centre of Barcelona, it can be quite easy to spot the houses designed by Gaudí because of their unique features. Casa Batlló has a façade decorated with glass and ceramics to look like the rippling surface of a lake with water lilies; Casa Vicens has ceramic tiles decorated with marigolds and other plant motifs on the cast-iron railings; and Casa Milà has an undulating limestone façade that is a constant curve that reflects the shape of the sea. There are also the mansion Palacio Güell and the crypt at the Colònia Güell church. Take the

time to look closely at each of them and you'll find symbolism in every little feature – like ventilation towers that look like warriors.

It's hoped that construction of La Sagrada Família will be finished by 2026, in time for the centenary of Gaudí's death (although that's looking unlikely). In the meantime, his body lies in the crypt of the basilica, at the heart of his greatest creation.

**01.** The Passion façade on the western side of the basilica tells the story of the Passion of the Christ **02.** When La Sagrada Família is finished, it should have 18 spires **03.** The columns and ceiling inside are designed to give the feeling of being in a forest

# Architects of World Heritage

While the works of hundreds of architects have been honoured with inclusion on the World Heritage List, there are some people who have been specially recognised by UNESCO with their name in the official title of a World Heritage Site.

Antoni Gaudí, with his buildings in Barcelona (*see* p. 130), is just one example. Another is the American architect, Frank Lloyd Wright, who left a legacy of more than 500 structures when he passed away in 1959. Eight of them have been included in the World Heritage Site, including **Unity Temple** in Oak Park, Illinois; the **Guggenheim** in New York City; and the famous **Fallingwater house** in Pennsylvania that was built over a waterfall.

The Swiss-French architect Le Corbusier, who passed away in 1965, has also been honoured with a World Heritage Site. A pioneer of modern architecture, his work stretches across the globe and the 17 places designated by UNESCO are found in seven countries. They include the **National Museum of Western Art** in Tokyo; the **Chandigarh Capitol Complex** in India; and the monastery of **Sainte Marie de La Tourette** near Lyon, France.

Four town houses in Brussels have been listed as a World Heritage Site, called the **Major Town Houses of the Architect Victor Horta**, bearing the name of the Belgian architect Victor Horta, who was one of the founders of the Art Nouveau movement towards the end of the 19th century. Nearby, in the Dutch city of Utrecht, a small home called the **Rietveld Schröder House**, designed by architect Gerrit Rietveld in 1924, is on the World Heritage List because of the innovative way it uses limited space for multiple purposes.

In Mexico City, the house and studio of 20th-century Mexican architect, Luis Barragán, has been turned into a museum. It reflects the bold and colourful designs he became famous for. **Casa Luis Barragán**, like many of the other masterpieces on the World Heritage List, is often visited by architectural students who find inspiration in works that continue to influence buildings across the globe.

Looking further back in time, the World Heritage Site called **Fortifications of Vauban** consists of 12 groups of fortified buildings along the western, northern, and eastern borders of France. They were designed by Sébastien Le Prestre de Vauban, a military engineer of King Louis XIV in the late 17th century. He created citadels, towers, sea forts, and even whole towns, and his ingenious military architecture was used for centuries.

The 16th-century architecture of Andrea Palladio is also recognised in a World Heritage Site bearing his name in the Italian city of **Vicenza**. His work was based on a detailed study of classical Roman design and the 23 buildings of his in Vicenza give the city a sense of grandeur. There are also 24 villas he designed across the Veneto region, creating a style that blended the countryside with ancient ideals.

National Museum of Western Art, Tokyo, Japan
**Inset** Sainte Marie de La Tourette, Lyon, France

# Rapa Nui (Easter Island)

## *Chile* (Inscribed 1995)

There aren't many inhabited places in the world as remote as Rapa Nui, also known as Easter Island. Created from volcanic rock, it has steep cliffs and rocky coves, with rich green grass thriving from regular downpours, but just scarce trees that are able to survive the blustery winds. Although it's officially part of Chile, it's actually 3500 kilometres (2175 miles) from the country's coastline. Just a small speck in the middle of the vast Pacific Ocean, the closest settled land is Pitcairn Island (a British Overseas Territory), 1921 kilometres (1194 miles) away.

Rapa Nui would be a geological fascination in any circumstance, but what makes it so special is the unique artwork that covers the island – the enormous statues, called moai, with elongated heads rising from the ground. The remoteness just adds to the marvel. Much of the great art around the world is the result of a gradual evolution of styles and cultural influences, but what the Rapa Nui people created here is theirs alone.

The figures in the statues stand stiff and alert, staring determinedly off into the distance, like

01

# Rapa Nui would be a geological fascination in any circumstance but what makes it so special is the unique artwork that covers the island.

eternal stone sentinels. Are they guarding the island, protecting its inhabitants, or maybe looking back to where they came from ... wherever that was? There is a lot of mystery about the Rapa Nui people, but the most common theories have them sailing across huge distances from another Polynesian island in about 1200 CE. The statues most likely represent their ancestors.

Across the island, there are about 900 of the statues. They range in height from 2 metres (6.5 feet) up to 20 metres (65 feet) and with heads almost the same size as their bodies. From the deep brow, a long nose slides down the face to a slight upward point. Long thin lips beneath the nostrils seem to purse, and beneath them is a firmly set square jaw that would be the envy of any action-movie hero. Although the features are relatively minimalistic, the statues manage to feel so alive and full of energy.

Easter Island is triangular in shape – about 25 kilometres long (15.5 miles) and 12 kilometres wide (7.4 miles) – with a landscape characterised by three large volcano craters. One of them, Rano Raraku, was the quarry for almost all of the moai. The statues were probably carved using picks made from hard basalt and then somehow moved into their positions. But about 400 moai are still in the quarry, in different stages of completion, as a visual journey through their creation.

**01.** A row of statues called moai are lined up along the coast, with the rugged cliffs of Rapa Nui (Easter Island) beyond them
**02.** It's thought the statues represent the ancestors of the people who carved them

# The Nazca Lines

## *Peru* (Inscribed 1994)

Were they done by aliens? That's one of the rather ridiculous theories about the enigmatic Nazca Lines in Peru – but you can see where it comes from. In the desert about 400 kilometres (248.5 miles) south of the capital Lima, these enormous shapes and patterns carved into the ground can only be truly appreciated from the sky. (Most tourists take a short scenic flight to see them properly.)

Or perhaps they were done *for* aliens? After all, one of the designs of a humanoid figure looks rather like an astronaut – and there shouldn't have been any of them around when these artworks were created at least 1500 years ago!

But, other than conspiracy theorists, most people agree the shapes were made by the Nazca culture between 500 BCE and 500 CE. While there are hundreds of geometric shapes and straight lines (the longest is 48 kilometres or 30 miles!), the figures of animals are the most interesting. A spider, a dog, a monkey, and a hummingbird, for instance, with the largest of these pictorials about 400 metres long (1312 feet). There's even a recently discovered mythical creature with spotted skin, multiple legs, and its tongue sticking out – part of the ancient magical–religious world the Nazca lived in.

The shapes were made by digging a shallow trench about 10 centimetres deep (4 inches), removing the dark red pebbles on the surface

and revealing the contrasting light clay beneath. The process was relatively easy, what was difficult was accurately creating a shape or making sure a line was straight. Many researchers believe the artists used the stars as a guide, and the patterns could even be an ancient map of the night sky. Perhaps the Nazca were helped by aliens ... indirectly, at least.

# While there are hundreds of geometric shapes and straight lines ... the figures of animals are the most interesting.

**01.** Some of the Nazca Lines are in the shape of animals, like this spider, while others are geometric or straight **02.** A viewing platform at the side of the road gives a sense of the size of some of the shapes in the desert **03.** One of the Nazca Lines is thought to look a bit like an astronaut!

# Who, when, where?

Although we often think of the UNESCO World Heritage List as a collection of places, it's important not to forget the people and the events behind them. Bricks and mortar only mean so much. It's normally their role in history that makes these cultural sites so significant.

Some of these places transcend more than just humanity in general. They are now defined by a single person or event, inextricably linked to that well-known narrative. The birthplace of an icon, the genesis of a revolutionary idea, the site of a natural disaster ... or even the site of a manmade disaster.

How long would it have taken to understand evolution if Darwin hadn't visited the Galápagos Islands (*see* p. 140), for example? Would we have anything like the Olympics if we didn't have the legacy of Olympia (*see* p. 142)? What would the world be like without Confucius in China (*see* p. 148), Buddha in Nepal (*see* p. 146), Nelson Mandela in South Africa (*see* p. 154), and Chief Roi Mata in Vanuatu (*see* p. 144)?

We still talk about these people and events decades or even centuries later and, though our view of them may have evolved over the years, each has had an incredible influence on the world. Visiting these sites is an opportunity to think about their legacy and the way they changed history ... for better or worse.

# Galápagos Islands

## *Ecuador* (Inscribed 1978)

The Galápagos tortoise has plenty of time to get to know its neighbours as it slowly lives its long life of well over 100 years. It will often see the marine iguana swimming by, the world's only ocean-going lizard. Just as it will often spot the Galápagos cormorant walking past, the only type of cormorant that has lost the ability to fly. It's a weird and wonderful collection of animals on the Galápagos Islands, which is exactly why these remote outcrops of land were so important to Charles Darwin, the father of evolution.

The Galápagos are made of an archipelago of 19 islands in the Pacific Ocean, 906 kilometres (563 miles) from the mainland of Ecuador, with a massive marine reserve around them.

Everywhere on the islands and in the water are huge groups of animals – hawks and penguins, seals and dolphins, crabs and snakes. Huge cacti grow between the rocks on the volcanic mountains, while daisy trees create a backdrop. There are about 600 species of native plants across the relatively arid landscapes of craters and rugged cliffs.

In 1831, at the age of 22, Darwin set off from England on board the *HMS Beagle* as the ship's naturalist for a five-year round-the-world trip to survey the coast of South America. The Galápagos Islands were not originally an official part of the journey and were only added in on the way home because there was time. Darwin was originally focused primarily on

01

02

geology, not biology, but while he was on the islands for about a month, he also studied the animals and noted peculiar things. For example, the mockingbirds were similar to the ones he had seen on the mainland, yet their features were slightly different on each island.

Darwin sailed away thinking about the strange animals he had seen, and was consumed with the idea of evolution. It wasn't until more than 20 years later, in 1859, that he published his

book, *On the Origin of Species* (you could argue that his views also evolved!). His theory that animals have gradually changed because of natural selection fundamentally upended the way science looked at the natural history of the world, rejecting the literal religious view of creation.

Most of the islands are still uninhabited (by humans, that is), although there are towns with accommodation options on a few of them: Santa Cruz, San Cristóbal, Floreana, and Isabela. However, most visitors to the Galápagos still travel like Charles Darwin – by boat – cruising between the different areas for around a week. It means that in this special melting pot of strange species, the humans are still the strangers.

01. The Galápagos tortoise lives for more than 100 years
02. Most of the Galápagos Islands are still uninhabited by humans 03. The marine iguana is the only lizard in the world that has adapted to also live in the ocean

# Olympia

*Greece* (Inscribed 1989)

It was noisy when I visited Olympia on a warm summer afternoon. Filling the air was the incessant buzz of insects, rising and falling like the roar of a crowd. Looking around the stadium, I imagined it filled with people – more than 45,000 could fit here – and, in my mind, the noise of the insects became the cheers of the Ancient Greeks.

It was here in 776 BCE that the first Olympic Games were held. The original stadium remains but it's incomparable to those of the modern games. It's just a dirt rectangle, 212 metres long (695 feet) and 28 metres wide (92 feet), with a natural grassy slope all around it. This is where the crowd would have sat to watch the competitions – running races, javelin throwing, or wrestling, perhaps. Much like recent Olympiads, new events were constantly added, and different types of chariot racing and boxing came later.

The ancient Olympic Games were held every four years as part of the Festival of Zeus, and more space at Olympia is dedicated to the king of the gods than to the sports. At the centre of the site was the Temple of Zeus, an enormous structure with 34 external Doric columns holding up the roof. The temple was 70 metres long (230 feet) and 20 metres high (66 feet), it housed the majestic Statue of Zeus, plated with gold and ivory, one of the Seven Ancient Wonders of the World.

The statue has long been lost (probably destroyed) and the temple sits in ruins, like much of the Olympia site, which is covered in green grass and shaded by large trees. But the original layout is clear and it's easy to find the Temple of Hera, slightly smaller than Zeus's temple, built about a century earlier. Several columns have been restored and it's here that the torch of the Olympic Flame is lit every four years and carried around the world to the next host city, continuing the connection to the movement's birthplace.

The ancient Olympic Games were held every four years as part of the Festival of Zeus, and more space at Olympia is dedicated to the king of the gods than to the sports.

**01.** The Philippeion was built in honour of Philip II of Macedon and is the only structure dedicated to a human **02.** Much of the Olympia site is in ruins, although you can still make out the original layout **03.** Many of the columns remain at the palaestra, which was part of a gymnasium

# Chief Roi Mata's Domain

## *Vanuatu* (Inscribed 2008)

In the traditional culture of Vanuatu, the deceased need to be prepared for the afterlife. It's why, when the great Chief Roi Mata died about 400 years ago, his supporters were so worried about his eternity that they buried at least 50 of his family members and followers with him. Alive.

Vanuatu may seem like an idyllic tropical utopia these days, around 80 lush green islands surrounded by crystal-clear water, where a relaxed pace of life harmoniously blends traditional culture with holiday resorts. But for many centuries there was constant conflict between the different tribes and clans of the islands. It was Chief Roi Mata who famously was able to bring peace to the main island of Efate in the 1600s through a series of initiatives, including large feasts where warring factions could discuss their issues. The moral values he espoused became an integral part of the Pacific nation's culture.

01

The World Heritage Site is made of three locations. On Efate island, there is the small village where Roi Mata lived, about an hour's drive from the capital Port Vila. Only 1.5 kilometres (0.9 miles) off the coast is the island of Lelepa and the place of Roi Mata's death (said to be at the hands of his brother, who clearly didn't care much for his peace feasts, and poisoned him at one, taking control himself). This location, known as Fel's Cave, has a small collection of rock art depicting weather patterns and local flora and fauna. The third location on the nearby island of Artok is the mass grave of Roi Mata. When he was buried there, it was declared forbidden land and it is still uninhabited, but the elaborate burial site was 'found' by French archaeologist

José Garanger in 1967 – who used local stories to determine its location – including the bodies of dozens of those who had been put in the ground alive.

One of the reasons the gravesite is so significant is that it proved the truth of the oral history that had been passed down through the generations. After centuries of intangible tales, now the landscape of Vanuatu also memorialises the deeds of Roi Mata. The illustrious chief is still revered by the country and his influence still felt across society.

Visually, this is not one of the most impressive World Heritage Sites you'll ever visit – even the burial site is just a few original artefacts amongst the dense green forest. But the Pacific nations are drastically underrepresented on the list of UNESCO sites (there are less than 10 out of more than 1100) and it's really important to have examples of the islands' cultures protected and accessible like this.

**01.** A tam tam in Chief Roi Mata's village, which makes a sound when struck, sending messages to surrounding areas **02.** The entrance to Fel's Cave on the island of Lelepa where Roi Mata was killed **03.** Vanuatu consists of 80 lush islands surrounded by tropical water

01

# Lumbini

## *Nepal* (Inscribed 1997)

With a full moon in the sky on a clear night in 623 BCE, Queen Mayadevi was walking back to her hometown in present-day Nepal to give birth ... when her baby came early. The stories say that as soon as the little boy was born, he walked seven steps to the north, looked around, then announced this would be his final rebirth. Those seven significant steps were just the first of what would become thousands more as he led a new movement. He started life being called Prince Siddhartha but, by the end, he was known simply as Buddha.

The spot where Buddha was born is called Lumbini and, although there was nothing there but sal trees and a pond at the time of his birth, it has grown over the centuries as one of the world's most important Buddhist pilgrimage sites. Amongst thick verdant forest are dozens

of monasteries where worshippers come to stay and meditate. Orange-robed monks stroll along paths and daytrippers ride boats up a long canal from the main entrance.

Lumbini became particularly popular during the Middle Ages, but was mostly lost and covered by trees from the 15th century. It was only towards the end of the 19th century that it was 'rediscovered' by archaeologists and, even then, it wasn't until 1978 that it had a major development into the site you'll find today, after UN Secretary-General U Thant (a Buddhist from Myanmar) visited in 1967 and was shocked by the state of disrepair.

The Lumbini Master Plan created a large new space with three sections, each exactly one mile long (1.6 kilometres). The first has tourist facilities, like hotels, shops and restaurants. The second section has the monasteries, each built by different countries or religious groups, the architecture and design representing their own style of Buddhism (for example, the Thai monastery is made from white marble, while

Myanmar's resembles Yangon's Shwedagon Pagoda). The final section has the modest Maya Devi Temple that protects a stone marking the exact birthplace of Buddha, along with a sacred pond where Queen Mayadevi is said to have purified her baby. It also has a sacred garden where light multi-coloured prayer flags hang from the branches and gently sway in the breeze above meditating monks.

The story of Buddha – much of it from historical sources rather than pure religious texts – tells of how Prince Siddhartha shrugged off his royal trappings and left his palace on a spiritual journey that would lead him to enlightenment. Visiting Lumbini replicates this path as you leave behind the hotels and shops, pass through the places of worship amongst the trees, and finish at the core of the faith.

**01.** Prayer flags blow in the breeze in the Sacred Garden around the Maya Devi Temple **02.** Dae Sung Shakya, the temple at the South Korean monastery, is one of the tallest at Lumbini **03.** The World Peace Pagoda was built by Japanese Buddhists **04.** Lumbini is an important pilgrimage site for Buddhists from across the world

# Temple, Cemetery and Mansion of Confucius

## *China* (Inscribed 1994)

In eastern China in 551 BCE, China's most famous philosopher was born. His surname was Kong and in time he would be referred to as Master Kong, which in Chinese is pronounced Kong Fuzi, a name that evolved into how he is best known – Confucius.

The ideals that Confucius developed 2500 years ago are still the foundations of Chinese society. At the core of his belief system was the notion that people should treat others the way they would want to be treated. Yet he also advocated for clear hierarchies within families and general society – children should respect their parents, wives their husbands, and the public

their rulers. In return, those with the power have a responsibility to care for the people who look up to them.

The lessons of Confucius were collected in a book called *The Analects* but it, like any of the ancient ideological texts, is read in different ways by different people. Confucianism spread from China to many other Asian countries and was used as the basis for various political and social systems, whether they were communist, democratic, capitalist, or socialist. At the World Heritage Site named in his honour, there are, along with many domestic visitors, large numbers of travellers from countries like South

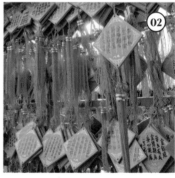

**01.** The Kong Family Mansion has grown enormous over the centuries **02.** Followers come from across the world to pay their respects **03.** A tranquil part of the Cemetery of Confucius **04.** There are more than 100,000 descendants buried in the Cemetery of Confucius

Korea, Japan, and Vietnam, where his legacy is still a part of daily life.

The site in Qufu consists of three main elements – the temple, mansion and cemetery. The original temple was founded in honour of Confucius in 478 BCE but it's been rebuilt many times since then and is now made up of more than 100 buildings. The Kong family mansion has also expanded massively in more than two millennia, and is now a grand aristocratic complex of 152 buildings. Much of the wealth came from Chinese emperors offering tributes to the family of Confucius. The cemetery is also huge and, along with the tomb of Confucius, it's said to contain the remains of more than 100,000 of his descendants.

Confucius would not recognise his home anymore, which has been transformed from a humble house into a sprawling estate full of motifs, including door studs, stone turtles and scenic openings. But you could probably say the same thing about his philosophy, which

has evolved as the world has modernised and his followers have applied it in different ways. One of the strongest beliefs held by Confucius was that we should worship our ancestors and honour the past – and that has clearly been embraced here.

# Famous birthplaces

The hospital where I was born has since been knocked down, so unfortunately it will never be named a World Heritage Site in my honour. But that was probably unlikely anyway, seeing as only a few people in history have had their place of birth become a UNESCO site for that reason (and none of them were travel writers).

Some of the most famous World Heritage Site birthplaces are of religious leaders, like Buddha at Lumbini (*see* p. 146). Near Jerusalem (*see* p. 86), there's the church in Bethlehem that has been identified since the 2nd century CE as the birthplace of Jesus. The **Church of the Nativity** on the site was first built in 339 CE and, although some of its original floor mosaics remain, the current complex is from the 6th century.

In **Assisi** in Italy, the town of Saint Francis's birth is a World Heritage Site, with the highlight being the enormous basilica named after him. With its arcades stretching out across the side of the hill, it's imposing from the outside; inside, it's covered in colourful frescoes.

Although much smaller, the **Church of the Ascension at Kolomenskoye** near Moscow in Russia was built in 1532 to celebrate the birth of a prince who would go on to become known as Ivan the Terrible. The first tsar of Russia, his story is violent and chaotic, but the church is calm and simple with a single white stone tower rising up like an octagonal tent.

In Mongolia, the sacred mountain of **Burkhan Khaldun**, crescent-shaped and usually snow-covered, is said to be the birthplace (and burial site) of Genghis Khan. The conqueror named the 2450-metre-high (8038-foot) peak as a sacred mountain in the 13th century and that was formalised by the country's government in 1955.

Of course, there are lots of other birthplaces that are World Heritage Sites, but that's not the main reason they're listed — just think of all those royal palaces and historic city centres, for instance. But I will point out one very notable omission when it comes to this topic, and that's the birthplace of the Prophet Muhammad and the most important place in Islam, **Mecca**.

It's also worth acknowledging that, although there is a decent representation in Europe and Asia, other continents don't have any World Heritage Sites marking the birthplaces of notable historical figures. It's another instance of the skewed nature of the World Heritage List. There are no birthplaces of women that have become World Heritage Sites either, an example of the broader issue of gender bias that UNESCO is now trying to remedy (*see* p. 202).

Basilica of Saint Francis of Assisi, Italy **Inset** The Church of the Ascension at Kolomenskoye, Russia

# Belém Tower

## *Portugal* (Inscribed 1983)

While Belém Tower was conceived as a tribute to Portuguese exploration, it is also a reminder of the colonialism that followed; a four-sided monument with two sides to the story. Its history may be controversial today, but there's an undeniable attraction to its architecture and setting.

Come down from the hills of Lisbon, with their retro trams and colourful tiled walls, walk along the Tagus River, and eventually you'll come to Belém Tower. Rising up from the

water just offshore, this limestone fortress with parapets and watch towers was built in 1514 to commemorate Vasco da Gama's epic voyage to India.

The location of Belém Tower was not arbitrary. It was from this spot that Portuguese sailors were heading off into the world on their voyages of exploration. But no trip had a more significant legacy than that of da Gama's. He found a maritime route around Africa from Europe to India which didn't just open up new trade opportunities, it also escalated the start of the global colonialism period that saw European powers compete to control the new lands they found on their voyages, often with devastating consequences for the original inhabitants.

The tomb of Vasco da Gama can be found just a kilometre (0.6 miles) away, in the Jerónimos Monastery, which makes up the World Heritage Site with Belém Tower. The night before he left on his voyage in 1497, da Gama and his crew sheltered and prayed in the ruins of an old church on the site. Although King Manuel I was already planning to replace it with the new monastery before da Gama even set sail, the new building was in some ways a tribute to the explorer, and was funded largely from taxes on the new trade with Africa and Asia.

When you visit, you can see why it took a century to build and cost so much. Jerónimos Monastery is one of the finest examples of Portuguese architecture and looking out through the detailed windows in the vast square cloister is a highlight, while the church

itself is full of artworks. It represents the beginning of the colonial era, not just because Vasco da Gama's body lies within it, but because it was built with the wealth that was amassed because of his voyage.

# Its history may be controversial today, but there's an undeniable attraction to its architecture and setting.

**01.** A queue of tourists waits on the walkway to go into Belém Tower **02.** Looking out from Belém Tower across the Tagus River **03.** The cloister at Jerónimos monastery is decorated with Manueline ornamentation

# Robben Island

## *South Africa* (Inscribed 1999)

Even under the sunny South African sky, Robben Island feels dark. This small collection of low-level buildings off the coast of Cape Town might not look like much, but for years it was a cage that tried to constrain the brightest of aspirations.

During the cruel period of apartheid in South Africa from 1948, while white leaders systemically discriminated against and segregated other races in the country, there was nobody who better represented the struggle for equality than Nelson Mandela. A leader in the revolutionary movement against apartheid, he was sentenced to life in prison in 1962, and only released in 1990 as the racist political system was collapsing. But, despite the decades of incarceration, Mandela would go on to be awarded the Nobel Peace Prize in 1993 (jointly with then President Frederik Willem de Klerk) and become South Africa's President in 1994.

Mandela spent 18 of his 27 years behind bars at Robben Island, a barren lump of land about 3 kilometres long (1.9 miles) and 2 kilometres wide (1.2 miles). The actual prison complex only covers about two per cent of the island's area and, even though it was technically maximum

01

security, the walls and the guard towers are not too tall – but being 7 kilometres (4.4 miles) from the mainland is a fairly big deterrent to escape. On other parts of the island are the cottages where the staff lived, and the quarries where prisoners were forced to work. Some of the quarries' rocks were used to build the entrance gate, which is adorned with the unsettling slogan 'we serve with pride'.

Walking through the old prison buildings – down the corridors of barred cells, into dormitories of uncomfortable metal beds – and hearing the stories from the guide (a former political prisoner), it's hard not to feel angry at how the government of the time treated people for even the slightest call for equality. But I still remember seeing the cell where Nelson Mandela was held and realising that such a small space was unable to contain the greatness of the man. The hope that justice would prevail was enough to motivate the prisoners to continue their campaigns for as long as

possible. Actively, if they could. Passively, if that was the only option. During the apartheid era, 12 political prisoners died on Robben Island.

Although Mandela may have been the most famous former prisoner, he was actually just one of three who would go on to become President of South Africa, the other two being Jacob Zuma and Kgalema Motlanthe. Knowing this affects the way you look at the complex that remains at Robben Island, and it stayed with me for a long time after the boat full of tourists returned us to the mainland. It's certainly a reminder of a shameful period of history, but it's also a symbol of the power and resilience of the human spirit.

**01.** Robben Island was used to hold prisoners until 1996
**02.** The walls of the prison didn't need to be too high because the rough waters surrounding the island acted as a barrier
**03.** One of the dormitories where prisoners slept on bunk beds

# Bikini Atoll

## *Marshall Islands* (Inscribed 2010)

It sounds like it could be an idyllic tourist hotspot. Sandy islands, covered in palm trees gently swaying in the wind, surrounding a calm blue lagoon – Bikini Atoll seems to have everything you could want from a South Pacific paradise. Yet these islands, about halfway between Hawaii and Australia, are not the kind of hotspot you want to visit. It was here that the United States of America conducted dozens of nuclear tests as it sought to build more powerful weapons in the global arms race during the Cold War.

If World War II saw the birth of the nuclear age, Bikini Atoll symbolises its childhood. Between 1946 and 1958, the United States carried out 67 nuclear tests – on the reef itself, on the sea, in the air, and underwater. In total, the force of all these tests was 7000 times as strong as the bomb the United States dropped on Hiroshima in 1945. You can see the physical legacy of these tests, with sunken ships at the bottom of the lagoon, and the enormous Bravo crater, which is 2 kilometres wide (1.2 miles) and 200 metres deep (656 feet). The crater was formed by the explosion of a weapon in 1954 that was two and half times stronger than expected, and which created a mushroom cloud 40 kilometres high (25 miles) and 100 kilometres wide (62 miles)!

The inhabitants of Bikini Atoll originally agreed to leave their islands temporarily in 1946 because the United States told them they would be able to safely return soon, but it became evident within months that their homeland had been devastatingly contaminated. Some that did return decades later suffered serious health problems. Eventually, over the 1970s and 1980s, the United States paid a total of about US$150 million in compensation.

## You can see the physical legacy of these tests, with sunken ships at the bottom of the lagoon

These days, there are few visitors but some divers make the journey to explore the coral reefs. Interestingly, scientists from Stanford University recently found that the marine ecosystem seems extremely healthy – partly because of the lack of human activity around the islands. But there are also some scientific theories that the animals may have developed ways to cope with the radiation, and this could be studied to help with human medicine – perhaps a chance for a site used to test weapons of death to eventually give life.

**01.** An underwater nuclear explosion known as Test Baker on 25 July, 1946 **02.** Divers explore the wrecks of sunken ships, including the Japanese battleship HIJMS *Nagato* and the American aircraft carrier USS *Saratoga* **03.** Scientists have been able to study the ecosystems around Bikini Atoll to assess the effect of the radiation

# Conflicted heritage

Most of the cultural sites on the World Heritage List celebrate great achievements of humankind – art, inventions, architecture, civilisation, faith. But there are a handful that protect examples of the dark side of our history. And there's a lot of controversy about whether that should be the case.

UNESCO itself has recently been looking at this issue and highlighted three World Heritage Sites associated with recent conflicts: the United States's nuclear testing site at Bikini Atoll in the Marshall Islands (*see* p. 156); the **Auschwitz–Birkenau** concentration camp run by Nazi Germany during World War II in Poland; and the **Genbaku Dome** in Japan that is a memorial to the atomic bomb dropped by the United States on Hiroshima in World War II. Using these examples, it's started a conversation about whether more places related to modern wars and horrific events should be included on the World Hertage List.

The main concerns about creating World Heritage Sites from sites of recent conflicts centre on who they represent and how they are defined. For example, different sides of a war may view the history very differently — internationally or even within the one country. Making one location a World Heritage Site and not another may simplify a complicated dispute and leave some communities aggrieved. It's also often the case that the narrative from these events continues to evolve for decades — or even centuries — afterwards.

Regardless, some countries are still pushing ahead with attempts to list conflict-related World Heritage Sites. These include the **Western Front cemeteries** in Belgium and France, and battle zones in Turkey (including **Gallipoli**) from World War I; the memorial complex of **Mamayev Kurgan** in Russia that commemorates the World War II Battle of Stalingrad; a series of mass graves at **Nyamata**, **Murambi**, **Bisesero**, and **Gisozi** that have become memorials to the 1994 genocide in Rwanda; and a torture camp at the **ESMA Site Museum** in Argentina that was used by the country's military junta between 1976 and 1983.

It's worth noting that in a discussion paper about 'recent conflicts' prepared for UNESCO in 2020, its advisory body, the International Council on Monuments and Sites (ICOMOS), did not include convict history, colonialism, and slavery, because it said that sites with those aspects are 'not focused primarily on negative memories, rather on the way the properties reflect in an outstanding way significant moments in, or shifts of, history'. However, this is another grey area and just shows there's no easy way to judge the sensitivities surrounding this complex issue.

Mamayev Kurgan, Russia **Inset** Auschwitz concentration camp, Poland

# Independence Hall

## *United States of America* (Inscribed 1979)

It was a sunny day of about 25°C (77°F), with clouds increasing in the afternoon, when representatives from the 13 American colonies met at the State House in Philadelphia on 4 July 1776. They were there to adopt the United States Declaration of Independence (but perhaps not sign it, as many people think – most historians believe that happened about a month later).

I mention the weather so you can try to imagine the scene when these representatives emerged from the Georgian-style red-brick building to address the crowd, reading to them for the first time the document that declared the United States of America was no longer under the control of the British Crown. 'We hold these truths to be self-evident, that all men are created equal ...' They were powerful opening lines, even if the men who wrote them didn't actually put them into practice.

Eleven years later, in 1787, delegates from the states met again at the building that would become known as Independence Hall from the

(01)

mid-1800s. This time, in rooms beneath a roof with no steeple (it had rotted and been removed), they wrote the US Constitution, a document designed to enshrine majority rule and safeguard minority rights. Exactly how successful that has been in the two centuries since is constantly debated, but there's no doubt it influenced a new style of democratic government across the world, with many countries using the document as the basis for their own constitutions.

The famous Liberty Bell is purported to have rung out when they read the Declaration of Independence, but back then it was just called the State House bell. It didn't take on any significance until the 1830s when the bell's inscription 'Proclaim Liberty Throughout All the Land Unto All the Inhabitants thereof' was adopted by the anti-slavery movement and the new name was first suggested. From the late 1800s, the bell was taken to expos around the country, but it now sits across the street

from where it originally hung, in a specially built structure where people can visit and see the important symbol of freedom in the United States.

Independence Hall is open to the public and visitors can line up in the morning to get a free ticket, first-come, first-served (how democratic!). Inside, the highlight is the Assembly Room, where the debates about the documents' drafting occurred. With white walls and two fireplaces at the front, the room has been recreated as it once was, full of tables covered in green cloth, with notebooks, quills and candles. It's relatively simple for one of the most historic rooms in the country, but I suppose it was the minds working here that are supposed to have added the brilliance.

**01.** Independence Hall was initially called the State House of Philadelphia **02.** The current clock tower was added to the building in 1828 **03.** The Liberty Bell, which originally hung in the steeple, is now on display in a specially built structure across the road from Independence Hall

# Pompeii

### *Italy* (Inscribed 1997)

Strolling along the streets, poking your head into shops, being welcomed into houses. There are public squares with official buildings, and residential suburbs sprawling out to the edges. It could be like walking through any other city – except that here in Pompeii, everything is 2000 years old, frozen in time (paradoxically) by the intense heat of an enormous volcanic explosion.

When Mount Vesuvius erupted in 79 CE, the nearby city of Pompeii was consumed, first by a toxic surge of gas and rock fragments, and then by falling ash and pumice. Within a couple of days, everything had been buried as it was at that moment, 6 metres deep (19 feet), not to be rediscovered until 1599 and then excavated properly for the first time from 1748. Did the eruption of Mount Vesuvius destroy Pompeii, or did it preserve it?

Certainly, the excavation of the site centuries later would have been like opening a time capsule. Pompeii was a relatively wealthy city, because of the fertile agricultural land around it. (The volcano that gives the rich land with one hand, takes away with the other.) It would have had a population of about 10,000 people, many of whom were able to escape when they felt the first effects of the eruption, although at least 1500 bodies have been found.

At its centre was the Forum, with the remains of the large Temple of Jupiter at the northern end (and Mount Vesuvius as a backdrop). While none of the buildings around the Forum have been restored, you can go in and get a sense of the Temple of Apollo, the Macellum, and the Basilica – the 68-metre-long (223-foot) imperial court where important legal and commercial meetings were held amongst its 38 imposing columns.

What makes a visit to Pompeii so fascinating is not the public buildings, but the private homes that you can wander through, hundreds of them lining the dozens of streets of the ancient city. The houses of the wealthier citizens are the most ostentatious (so, not much has changed in two millennia) and you can see beautiful frescoes at the House of Sirico, a powerful man with trade and political connections, with mythological subjects inspired by the Trojan War painted on the walls. Yet there's beauty in the small things as well – at the House of the Tragic Poet, a small mosaic of his pet includes the words 'Beware of the dog'. Such a common timeless sign reminds us that this special city was once so normal.

# It could be like walking through any other city – except that here in Pompeii, everything is 2000 years old, frozen in time (paradoxically) by the intense heat of an enormous volcanic explosion.

**01.** The view across the forum at Pompeii to Mount Vesuvius **02.** Before it was buried by the volcanic explosion, Pompeii would've had a population of about 10,000 people **03.** Many of the homes of wealthy residents were decorated with vibrant frescoes

# The natural world

Even the most dazzling of humanity's creations pale in comparison to the work of nature, the planet's greatest artist and architect. Impressive in its vastness and absorbing in its detail, the beauty of the natural world never ceases to amaze. About a quarter of the UNESCO World Heritage List consists of natural sites and, combined, they protect over 3.7 million square kilometres (1.43 million square miles), just less than one per cent of the world's surface.

From the enormous mountains of the Himalayas (*see* p. 166), to the Grand Canyon (*see* p. 174) carved across the land; from the intensity of Iceland's volcanoes (*see* p. 190) to the power of South America's Iguazu Falls (*see* p. 180); it's the diversity of the world's natural wonders that particularly awe and inspire.

It's not just the landscapes that are extraordinary, it's also the ecosystems that thrive within them, the fascinating plants and animals – from the migrating wildebeest of the Serengeti (*see* p. 168), to the deadly Komodo dragons of Indonesia (*see* p. 172), and the hundreds of coral species in the reefs of our oceans (*see* p. 186).

Many natural wonders are under threat from environmental pressures, and even from the tourists who come to marvel at their beauty. Protecting and promoting their fragility in a sustainable way has never been more important.

# Mount Everest

*Nepal* (Inscribed 1979)

There are approximately eight billion people on the planet, but only about six thousand of us have ever been to the top of it. As alluring as it is dangerous, Mount Everest has long been seen as the pinnacle of a mountaineer's ambitions. At 8848 metres (29,028 feet) from sea level, the highest mountain in the world, it is both a natural wonder and a symbol of human accomplishment.

The first people known to reach the summit of Mount Everest were New Zealander Edmund Hillary and Nepali–Indian Tenzing Norgay in 1953. Since then, the climb has become much easier – although still very risky – and hundreds reach the summit each year, taking about five days for a return trip from base camp, which is at an altitude of 5364 metres (17,598 feet). (However, the entire expedition – including trekking to the base camp, acclimatising, and waiting for the right weather – can take about two months.) Along with the mountaineers, there are also several hundred professional local guides who will annually prepare the route with ropes and ladders, climb up to leave provisions in camps along the way, and then escort adventurers to the top. Climbing Mount Everest has become big business and, ironically, there are now fears of overtourism in one of the world's most inaccessible locations!

From a distance, Mount Everest may appear as a hulking monolith, but it has endless little details, from glaciers creeping down its slopes,

01

01. Hundreds of climbers reach the summit of Mount Everest each year 02. Climbers spend time at Everest Base Camp, with an altitude of 5364 metres (17,598 feet), to acclimatise before heading to the summit 03. There are seven mountains over 7000 metres (22,965 feet) in Sagarmatha National Park

snow as hard as rocks, and barren rocky patches. Climbers will tell you it's constantly changing, best exemplified by the Khumbu Icefall, a jumble of huge blocks of ice that crack open to create new crevices that mountaineers must traverse. On the higher elevations, there are almost no plants or animals (only humans seem foolish enough to want to be at this altitude!).

Although Mount Everest gets all the attention, it is actually part of a larger World Heritage Site called Sagarmatha National Park. Mount Sagarmatha is the name Nepal gave to Mount Everest about a century after the British named it in 1865 for George Everest, a Surveyor General of India. (To his credit, Everest argued against using his name for the mountain because locals had trouble pronouncing it.) Within the national park, there are seven peaks over 7000 metres (22,965 feet),

giant staircases to the sky. At the park's lowest point, 2845 metres (9333 feet), dense green alpine forests cover the slopes, drinking up the fresh water that flows from the snow caps above them. Hidden amongst the trees are snow leopards and red pandas.

Along with the protected status of the area, one of the main reasons the mountains have been so well conserved is because of the local inhabitants. About 6000 Sherpas live in 20 villages where their ancestors have been for at least 400 years, special genetic factors allowing them to live more easily at the high altitudes. Despite the influx of foreigners who come for the summit's challenge, the villagers have largely continued their traditional cultural and religious practices, which include restrictions on hunting animals. With the mountains in their DNA, they are the caretakers of the top of the world.

# The Serengeti

## *Tanzania* (Inscribed 1981)

The wildebeest, all two million of them, are the first to begin the spectacular annual migration across the Serengeti, the enormous trail of animals stark against the vast yellow plains. These grasslands are sparse and dry and it's easy to spot the animals, with few places to hide except the occasional umbrella-like acacia tree or the small granite outcrops known as kopjes. With a long face and stocky head leading an explosion of taut skin and bones, a wildebeest looks athletic rather than smart, but they are clever enough to stay together in large tight groups to make it harder for their predators – because not far behind the wildebeest are lions and hyenas, looking for an easy meal. If the hunters are still hungry once the leaders of the migration have passed

through, hundreds of thousands of gazelles and zebras will come along next.

This migration of millions of animals is a tumultuous war between carnivores and herbivores, where battles are won every day but neither side ever really loses. The hooves of the wildebeest, gazelles, and zebras throw up the dry dirt of the savannah until they reach fresh grass, newly watered by the wet season. The lions and hyenas pick off the younger, slower animals (perhaps also the most tender?) but, with 400,000 wildebeest calves born each year before the migration, it's hardly a dent in the herd. The most dramatic moments tend to come when the animals need to cross rivers en masse and thousands of crocodiles make the most of it, the frantic splashing of the panicked crowd turning the brown water white.

Of course, not all animals in Serengeti National Park migrate and, amongst the flat grasslands dotted with rocky outcrops, there are also giraffes, hippos, warthogs, and monkeys. Four of the species in the park are listed as threatened or endangered – the black rhino, leopard, cheetah, and African elephant. Although poaching has been a problem in the park in the past, recent conservation efforts like aerial patrols, community outreach programs, and de-snaring projects have seen increases in animal numbers and about 30 per cent of Tanzania is now protected land.

The migrating animals pass across the Serengeti from April to July, when they move into the Maasai Mara game reserve in Kenya (an area that the national government is hoping will become a World Heritage Site soon). They will feed there for several months before following the rains back through woodlands towards waterholes on the south-eastern side of Serengeti National Park, a total journey of about 800 kilometres (500 miles). Here, the females will give birth and, when the weather changes, they will start out on the route once more. The thing with migrations is that they are endless. The wildebeest will go around again and the predators will be there again, with the circle of life in the African plains continuing on as always.

**01.** A herd of impala run through grasslands of Serengeti National Park **02.** Recent conservation efforts have led to an increase in animal numbers in the Serengeti **03.** A lioness and her cub follow a trail in the national park

Wildebeest crash through the water on their annual migration across the Serengeti

# Komodo National Park

## *Indonesia* (Inscribed 1991)

The Komodo dragon, a deadly and ancient reptile, exists on just four small Indonesian islands, isolated from the rest of the planet, ensuring its survival for the past 20 million years. It had no predators and, quarantined and indomitable, evolution largely overlooked these killers. It was not until 1910 that they were revealed to the Western world. Like a cross between a lizard and a crocodile, they can grow up to 3 metres long (almost 10 feet). At first glance, they seem docile and slow but, when I saw one run, I felt my heart skip a beat. They are fast. And when they bite, you can hear the snap of their powerful jaws.

The islands of the national park seem imbued with a tropical ambience – white sandy beaches and clear water full of vibrant coral. But go further inland and there are about 5700 Komodo dragons in the national park, hidden in rugged hillsides of dry savannah and thorny green vegetation. This is where they work together to find their prey – mainly deer, buffalo, goats, and birds. Sometimes they can attack and eat

01

the whole animal right there. Other times they will bite and then wait patiently. Their saliva contains bacteria that will eventually kill, so they will stalk their prey for up to three weeks until it dies and can be devoured.

You might think living on a small island with thousands of prehistoric killer reptiles would be scary, but the small community in Komodo National Park is relatively relaxed – humans are not the main food source for the Komodo dragons. Sometimes, though, that doesn't matter, as a ranger called Maen found out one day when he came into work at his wooden hut and sat down, not realising the door had been left open overnight and a Komodo dragon had slipped in and was waiting under his desk.

This is what Maen told me when I met him at the park: 'I tried to pull my leg but the dragon followed and I look and see a tail moving over there. And I think this is a problem for me. I pull my leg too fast and it got trapped in the table and then the dragon bite.'

Maen managed to pull his leg free from the jaws but his hand got bitten in the process. Other rangers rushed to the hut but so did other dragons, drawn by the smell of blood. Maen's colleagues had to fight them off as they rushed him to a boat and then a hospital, where he had six hours of emergency treatment.

The islands of Komodo National Park are not a zoo and all the animals you'll see are wild. Yet, some have become comfortable with humans and will wander through the community. As a visitor, you'll always have a ranger with you, yet their only defence is a long-forked stick to hold the animals at bay. As one ranger warned me: 'When they are aggressive, that's not enough. Then we have to run.' I'm sure poor Maen wishes he'd had that option.

**01.** The Komodo dragons are able to wander into the small community that lives permanently on the island **02.** Komodo dragons can stalk their prey for days once they have bitten it **03.** The beautiful islands of Komodo National Park were isolated from the rest of the world for millennia

# The Grand Canyon

## *United States of America* (Inscribed 1979)

Like an enormous scar across the face of Arizona, the Grand Canyon is worthy of all its dramatic superlatives. While not the largest canyon in the world, it's certainly one of the most spectacular, its abrupt rim and striking red cliffs making it a symbol of America's Wild West. The huge width and depth dwarf anything that comes across it, and many who have tried to conquer it have been bettered.

It took six million years of geologic activity to create the foundations of the canyon, while the tumbling Colorado River did the rest, slowly carving out the shape you see today. The Grand Canyon twists and turns for 445 kilometres (276 miles) and is about 1.5 kilometres (0.9 miles) deep for much of its course. At its narrowest point, it's just 500 metres (0.3 miles) across, while it stretches to 30 kilometres (18 miles) at its widest.

One of the most striking elements of the Grand Canyon are the shapes that rise up from within the path of the erosion, like stone spires between the rims on either side, worshipped by the crowds of visitors who gaze out from viewing platforms. These mountains, like the sides of the canyon, have layers of different colours that change with the depth – from orange at the top, to vermillion, then purple and pink, down to brown and grey – creating a visual gradient of billions of years of the planet's history. More than just beautiful, it is a priceless research tool for geologists who can study all four eras of the earth's evolution.

While geological history is told in billions of years, human history is told in thousands, and the canyon has influenced human life here for at least 10,000 years – one of the reasons it is a World Heritage Site. First it was hunters and gatherers who would move along the edges of precipices and down into the great corridors of stone, catching animals such as mammoths and giant sloths. Artefacts discovered in the region show how, as animals got smaller over the millennia, so did the spear tips.

Eventually people began to settle on the land, carving granaries into the canyon's walls and decorating caves with art. Although it's believed a natural event like a drought forced the inhabitants to leave the canyon area about 700 years ago, new groups moved in about a century later. From those ancestors, there are 11 current First Nations' tribes that have historic connections to the land within the Grand Canyon National Park. You can camp near beautiful waterfalls on the land of one of the tribes by hiking a 13-kilometre-long (8-mile) trail to the Havasupai Indian Reservation.

While geological history is told in billions of years, human history is told in thousands, and the canyon has influenced human life here for at least 10,000 years.

**01.** The layers of the Grand Canyon's cliffs change colour, reflecting different eras of geological history **02.** There are more than 20 official day-hike trails in Grand Canyon National Park **03.** The Grand Canyon Skywalk, opened in 2007, is owned by the Hualapai nation

# The Rocky Mountains

## *Canada* (Inscribed 1984)

Although the mighty Rocky Mountains stretch for about 4800 kilometres (3000 miles) from New Mexico up to the Canadian provinces of Alberta and British Columbia, it's only the section in Canada that has been designated as a World Heritage Site. It's here, in the colder northern extremes, that you'll find striking landscapes of stoic glaciers that have survived for centuries, snow-covered peaks that begin the water's journey to cascades below, and canyons filled with tall trees that hide the entrances to caves.

At first I thought the name a bit silly (from my experience, all mountains are rocks!) but when I finally visited, I realised the name of the Rocky Mountains was perfect. The highest peaks – many of them well above 3000 metres (9842 feet) – have barely any vegetation at the top, just bare stone and snow. The browns and whites of the high altitudes contrast with the lush green forests and energetic blue rivers of the lower altitudes, where the elk and moose live with bears, both black and grizzly.

One of the best ways to experience the Canadian Rockies is by driving the Icefields Parkway, a 233 kilometre (144 mile) stretch of road that connects Jasper and Banff National Parks. With waves of mountains on either side,

01

the road hugs a fast-flowing river, and new landscapes are revealed around each bend. Along the way are highlights like Jasper's Athabasca Falls, where the water tumbles over enormous boulders, and Banff's Bow Glacier Falls, with white cascades flowing down a bare cliff-face.

In the centre is the crowning glory, the Columbia Icefield, the largest ice field in all the Rockies, feeding six major glaciers. You can walk up to the leading edge of the Athabasca Glacier, which often seems to act as a runway for the wind. Although it's about 6 kilometres long (3.7 miles), unfortunately it is receding about 5 metres (16 feet) a year.

**01.** The Icefields Parkway connects Jasper and Banff National Parks, past glaciers and mountains **02.** The dramatic Athabasca Falls in Jasper National Park **03.** Many of the Rocky Mountains are covered in snow in the colder months of the year

# National Parks as World Heritage Sites

These days it seems normal (even obligatory) that we protect tracts of nature from human interference, but that wasn't always the case.

It wasn't really until the 1800s that people started to think about conservation of forests, although that was mainly about the economics of a sustainable timber industry in places like British-controlled India. It wasn't until a few decades later, in the United States of America, that there was a historic move to protect land for the good of the future, with environmentalists lobbying the government to declare **Yellowstone** the world's first national park in 1872. It began a movement that has now seen about half the world's countries create national parks (other countries have different forms of protection, it should be noted) and more than a hundred of them are also World Heritage Sites, meaning countries need to regularly defend conservation practices to UNESCO. Although having both National Park and World Heritage designations doesn't change much in practice, it does perhaps elevate them to the non-existent status I like to call an 'international park'.

The oldest one in Africa is **Virunga National Park** in the Democratic Republic of Congo, which was created in 1925 to protect the mountain gorillas; while the continent's highest mountain is protected by Tanzania's **Kilimanjaro National Park**.

Vietnam's **Phong Nha-Ke Bang National Park** has the world's largest cave (Son Doong Cave); you'll find the world's tallest waterfall (Angel Falls) in Venezuela's **Canaima National Park**; there's the longest underground river in the world at the **Puerto-Princesa Subterranean River National Park** in the Philippines; and Tajikistans's **Tajik National Park** has the world's longest non-polar glacier (Fedchenko Glacier).

National parks conserve areas like the strange turret landscape of Turkey's **Göreme National Park**; the enormous 7500-metre-high (24,606-foot) volcano in the **Teidei National Park** on the Spanish island of Tenerife; and the imposing glaciers across several national parks in New Zealand's **Te Wāhipounamu** (*see* p. 43) site.

The World Heritage Site status doesn't just add another level of natural protection through international oversight, it's an acknowledgement of the human understanding that it's our job to do that.

# *Although having both National Park and World Heritage designations doesn't change much in practice, it does perhaps elevate them.*

Phong Nha-Ke Bang National Park, Vietnam
**Inset** Virunga National Park, Democratic Republic of Congo

# Iguazu Falls

### *Argentina and Brazil* (Inscribed 1984 and 1986)

You hear Iguazu Falls (Iguazú in Spanish and Iguaçu in Portuguese) before you see them, the crashing roar of water hurtling over cliffs at high speed and then smashing into the river below. What makes the sound so deafening is that it's not just one waterfall, but a series of up to 275 of them (the exact number changes depending on rainfall), cascading over cliffs on both sides of a canyon. Together they create the world's largest and most visually impressive waterfall complex, taller than Niagara and much wider than Victoria. It's easier to picture the layout of Iguazu Falls from the sky, when you see the upstream section of the Iguazu River getting wider and slower as it approaches the start of the canyon and fills the space on every side of it, before crashing over the cliffs.

## 02

It's why visiting can be an overwhelming experience at first. The canyon straddles a border, one side in Brazil and the other in Argentina, requiring you to choose where you'll access it from – to do both involves a 40 kilometre (24 mile) trip back through two towns and all that comes from an international border crossing. Walking along either side, you'll have waterfalls thundering down around you, and then a view across to the row of white curtains on the other. As you approach the start of the canyon, the noise of the falls gets louder, until you came face-to-face with the tallest section, known as the Devil's Throat, where torrents of water crash from a height of 80 metres (262 feet) into the chasm of mist below.

Visiting Iguazu Falls can take days, especially if you venture a bit deeper into the forests of the national parks to try to spot rare animals like jaguars, giant otters, and giant anteaters. Because, as well as the scale being unlike any other waterfall on earth, the effect of the almost-permanent spray in the air is felt across the ecosystem, with lush and dense flora flourishing and attracting more than 400 bird species to the 80 types of trees.

Unusually, the waterfalls are covered by two World Heritage Sites – Iguazú National Park in Argentina (inscribed in 1984) and Iguaçu National Park in Brazil (inscribed in 1986). These days, UNESCO encourages countries to submit combined nominations to avoid this kind of bureaucratic confusion.

**01.** Iguazu Falls is made up of a series of 275 waterfalls
**02.** Water crashes over the cliffs on both sides of the river
**03.** The waterfalls create a constant mist, which supports the surrounding ecosystem

# Ha Long Bay

## *Vietnam* (Inscribed 1994)

The jewel of Vietnam's coast, Ha Long Bay, glitters in the sun, the light dancing off the turquoise water. Across the bay are 1600 islands and islets, a landscape of limestone karst peaks emerging from the water. From a distance they look like an armada of stone and, closer, like the tips of Neptune's trident being held aloft. The hundreds of islands are each a different size and shape and there seems no logic to their placement in a jumble in every direction, creating the effect of an enchanting natural maze.

Lush foliage grows from the rocky islands, the dusting of green giving homes to birds and other small animals. Almost all except the biggest islands are uninhabited by humans. That doesn't mean there aren't lots of people in Ha Long Bay, though. As one of the country's most popular sites, the waters are filled with boats carrying tourists. There was a time when these junks left their junk in the water and the bay faced serious environmental concerns, but restrictions since 2013 have seen the health of the site improve remarkably. Although the Vietnamese Government understands the importance of protecting its national icon, there has also been some pressure (and financial assistance) from UNESCO to improve the management of the site.

01

I noticed the change on my most recent visit to Ha Long Bay. It had been almost a decade since I had been – back then the boats had criss-crossed all over the bay, people jumped in the water everywhere to swim (and wash), while food scraps and other rubbish was casually thrown overboard from the floating kitchens. Now the boats must follow a limited number of routes with designated areas for swimming (and, of course, rubbish must be taken back to the mainland).

An overnight boat trip leaving from Ha Long Bay's mainland is still the best way to experience its islands, slowly cruising amongst the limestone pillars, seeing the colours of the

water and the stone change with the arc of the sun. In the stillness of the night, sounds drift across the surface and echo off the cliffs, and with a full moon, Ha Long Bay sparkles. Tour companies offer a wide range of cruise options, but there's something quite humbling about knowing that, regardless of a boat's prestige, everyone on the water has the same view.

# Across the bay are 1600 islands and islets, a landscape of limestone karst peaks emerging from the water.

**01.** Limestone karst peaks covered in green vegetation rise from the water of Ha Long Bay **02.** The large number of cruises is now better managed to reduce the impact on the environment **03.** There are about 1600 islands across Ha Long Bay

# Phoenix Islands Protected Area

## *Kiribati* (Inscribed 2010)

In the centre of the Pacific Ocean, beyond tropical and past paradise, is the island nation of Kiribati, a country so remote that most people don't even know how to pronounce its name (it's ki-rah-bahss). It's made up of 33 islands scattered across an expanse of ocean about the same dimensions as the contiguous United States of America, although the official boundaries of the country only include a fraction of that area. Still, Kiribati is the only nation in all four hemispheres.

But it's not the land that's the focus for the country's World Heritage Site, it's the huge tract of water around the Phoenix Islands (one of the country's three main island groups). Around these islands is a pristine deep-sea environment where you'll find one of the world's best coral archipelago ecosystems. Far away from all of the environmental hazards of major human industries, the underwater world has thrived here in perfect balance, the area home to about 200 coral species, 500 fish species, and 18 types of marine mammals. Scientists assume there are many more animals to discover here in the future as researchers look deeper (literally).

For people accustomed to hiking on land, it may seem strange to describe the ocean as 'wilderness', but it's one of the best words for

01

the Phoenix Islands Protected Area. Under the water, there are 14 known volcanoes, now extinct, that rise up from the sea floor like mountains. The colourful blooms of coral create forests that cover the reefs and provide homes for the small fish darting amongst them. Sharks float silently looking for prey, turtles cruise through on their migrations, dolphins frolic in the lagoons, the birds circle and squawk in the air above. Out here in the middle of nowhere, there's a whole lot of something going on.

The area was the largest of any World Heritage Site on the planet when it was added in 2010, its 408,000 square kilometres (157,529 square miles) about the same size as California. But it was overtaken in 2019 by a new World Heritage Site called French Austral Lands and Seas, based around a group of volcanic islands near Antarctica famous for their marine birds.

However, the enormous size of the Phoenix Islands is important, not as a competition, but because it guarantees an unspoiled swathe of the world for the important marine life below its surface. Its remoteness ensures only a handful of humans will see it each year – and that's what keeps it so special.

**01.** The pristine waters around the Phoenix Islands have been protected partly because they are so remote
**02.** The Phoenix Islands have one of the world's best coral archipelago ecosystems

# Underwater heritage

While we tend to think of places on the World Heritage List as being on land, there are actually dozens of World Heritage Sites that are underwater, just like the Phoenix Islands Protected Area in Kiribati (see p. 184). Known for their outstanding ecosystems, iconic biodiversity and exceptional variety of habitats, scientists are focused on the conservation of these sites. Many of us will never see these places in person, but the protected areas give researchers greater opportunities to study the wonderlands beneath the surface.

The most famous underwater site is probably the **Great Barrier Reef**, the world's largest reef system that stretches for 2300 kilometres (1429 miles) off the east coast of Australia. On the country's west coast is another remarkable reef called **Ningaloo** that can be accessed directly from the beach. The world's second-largest coral reef, the **Belize Barrier Reef**, is also a World Heritage Site and has about 450 islands along its length.

In the South Pacific, the **Rock Islands Southern Lagoon** in Palau is protected because of the unique coral reefs that have formed in the turquoise waters around the mushroom-shaped limestone islands; the marine park around the **Cocos Island** in Costa Rica is on the list because of the diversity it offers divers in tropical waters; and **Tubbataha Reef** in the Philippines is remarkable for its pristine coral reef with a spectacular 100 metre (328 foot) perpendicular wall.

In the French territory of **New Caledonia**, a series of lagoons has been designated a World Heritage Site because of the abundance of marine animals, particularly the large population of dugongs. The protection of dugongs is also one of the main reasons the Sudanese site of **Sanganeb** in the Red Sea has been listed. The whale sanctuary of **El Vizcaino** off the west coast of Mexico was added to the World Heritage List because it's considered to be the world's most important spot for the breeding of the North Pacific Grey Whale.

With climate change affecting the oceans at an unprecedented rate, coupled with other issues like pollution and overfishing, it has never been more important to protect the world's marine sites.

*Many of us will never see these places in person, but the protected areas give researchers greater opportunities to study the wonderlands beneath the surface.*

Belize Barrier Reef, Belize **Inset** Sanganeb, Sudan

# Plitvice Lakes

### *Croatia* (Inscribed 1979)

The Plitvice Lakes stretch along an 8 kilometre (4.9 mile) landscape, 16 of them almost touching, one after another, lustrous like a string of pearls in a necklace. But once, there were no lakes here, just water flowing unimpeded. It flowed above ground, and it flowed through the rocks below ground – and this is how the story of Plitvice Lakes begins. The rock the water was passing through was limestone, and over time the calcium carbonate was stripped from the ground and mixed with the water. Much of it just washed away into greater Croatia, but some got deposited along the way, perhaps on previous deposits, until eventually enough calcium carbonate created a dam wall ... and a new lake.

The end result is what you can see today with each of the lakes interconnected to the other, the flow of the water beginning at the higher end and gradually moving down lake by lake, sometimes underground, but often over the top of a lake's edge, creating thin drapes of waterfalls that appear between bushes and trees. They spill over into the pools of water that each have a distinctive colour, from the green of emerald to the blue of sapphire, along with a few shades of turquoise.

Up close to the lakes, they're so clear you can see fish swimming, but the higher vantages give a dazzling vista of this water playground.

The pools look so inviting, and it's no surprise people want to dive into them, but the fragile ecosystem is easily damaged so swimming has been banned since 2006. Instead, you can walk along elevated wooden boardwalks that snake around the sides of the lakes, across the travertines, and occasionally cut across the crystalline water itself. In total, there are more than 18 kilometres (11 miles) of pathways in the national park, connecting the different bodies of water and leading up to viewpoints at the top of the cliffs. Up close to the lakes, they're so clear you can see fish swimming, but the higher vantages give a dazzling vista of this water playground, where the cascades seem to emerge out of nowhere and paint the walls in a way that might appear magical.

**01.** Visitors can't swim at Plitvice Lakes but elevated walkways lead you amongst the pools **02.** The lakes are just one part of a picturesque landscape amongst steep cliffs and lush foliage **03.** Water flows downstream through the rocks and over the edges of the lakes

# Vatnajökull National Park

## *Iceland* (Inscribed 2019)

This truly is the land of ice and fire, where two of nature's extremes meet to face battle. Stretching across Iceland's Vatnajökull National Park is the largest glacier in Europe, blanketing canyons and mountains as it rises from an altitude of about 300 metres (984 feet) up to 2000 metres (6561 feet) above sea level. The icecap seems so solid and enormous, covering about 10 per cent of the country, there's only one thing that can wound it – the volcanoes that are hidden beneath its white surface.

Volcanic eruptions of molten lava explode into the frozen landscape and split open the ancient glaciers, reshaping the landscape in just moments. The Icelanders even have a name for it – jökulhlaup – a sudden flood caused by the breach of the margin of a glacier during an eruption. It's happened so many times over history, and the combination of lava and floods has repeatedly carved out new canyons and river systems.

To understand the intensity of the explosions, head to the geological scar across the ground at the Lakagíga fissure in the western part of Vatnajökull National Park, which caused one of recent history's largest volcanic eruptions

01

between 1783 and 1784. It was so powerful it changed global weather patterns, leading to crop failures across Europe, drought in India, and snowstorms in the United States of America. So just imagine what it can do to a bit of land here in Iceland.

The dynamism of the ice and fire shouldn't scare away visitors, though. In fact, it's what makes Vatnajökull National Park so enthralling. Around the glacier itself are large river systems with powerful waterfalls, and geothermal areas where the colours of minerals bubble. You can hike up mountains, walk in green fields, climb into ice caves – and all the while volcanoes will watch you from the horizon, silent for now, waiting to make their next move.

**01.** Vatnajökull is the largest glacier in Europe, with a surface area of about 8100 square kilometres **02.** Much of the national park is covered in ice, which can be explored independently or with guides **03.** Continual volcanic activity over many years has shaped the landscape in the park

# Science and technology

Behind every great leap forward of the human race, there is usually a momentous achievement in science or technology. The invention of the wheel, the ability to harvest crops, ships that could sail across oceans, machines that could mass produce. Many of these moments are hard to pinpoint in history, but some of the places that reflect the accomplishments have been recognised as UNESCO World Heritage Sites.

There are ancient examples of technology in agriculture at Croatia's Stari Grad Plain (*see* p. 216) and aquaculture at Budj Bim in Australia (*see* p. 218), impressive not just for their ingenuity but because they were used for thousands of years. In Belgium, the printing presses at the Plantin-Moretus Workshops (*see* p. 208) spread information around the world, while the enormous salt mine at Wieliczka in Poland (*see* p. 196) gives us a deeper look into the lives of its workers. New technology at a Japanese silk mill (*see* p. 200) helped modernise the country's whole economy, and an observatory in England (*see* p. 198) let us see further into the universe than ever before.

Science, technology, and the industries that go with them can often leave permanent scars in the earth, but they are reminders of the scientific advancements that built our modern world.

# Völklingen Ironworks

## *Germany* (Inscribed 1994)

The Industrial Revolution, beginning in the late 18th century in Britain, changed the world and created the foundations for the modern society we live in today. These huge changes were built on iron and, although it took some decades for the technology to reach Germany, the country quickly became an industrial powerhouse, with Völklingen eventually becoming the most productive ironworks in Europe.

Völklingen Ironworks was established in 1873 and was expanded over the years until the 1930s, after which there were no major changes to the site. Operations didn't stop at Völklingen Ironworks until 1986 and now it's open to the public, with a heritage trail that leads visitors through all parts of the complex. Pipes, steel tracks, huge silos, and mashings of machines fill the site, like a metal jungle with neither beginning nor end. The light breaks through in places but, otherwise, the sun is eclipsed by constructions in every direction, seemingly haphazard but, of course, all part of a considered production line. In the sprawling industrial patchwork, you feel so insignificant. At its peak in the 1960s, the ironworks had 17,000 people working here – and you can only imagine the noise that must have boomed from every direction, and the heat when all the machines were operating.

Visitors can see every stage of the pig-iron production process, from the sintering shed, through the burden shed, up to the coking plant. There are more than 6 kilometres (3.7 miles) of paths to follow, a maze that offers detours up metal staircases, past gondolas hanging from rails, along tracks surrounded by weeds, and to platforms with views across the terrain of hardware.

Most similar plants to Völklingen were demolished when they were closed – people saw little heritage value in them and the metal could be better used elsewhere. So it's quite remarkable we have a complete ironworks left to see, the only intact example in Western Europe and North America, in fact. (It's worth noting that the location for the first successful smelting of iron ore with coke at Ironbridge in the UK is also a World Heritage Site.)

Throughout its history, Völklingen Ironworks was used to make steel for railway tracks then, as the industrial age gathered pace, girders for building construction. During the World Wars, the steel was used for weapons and, afterwards, for reconstruction. Even by-products of making iron, like fertiliser and tar, became important for the economic success of the company and the continent.

In 1994, Völklingen Ironworks became the first industrial site in any country to be listed as a World Heritage Site, a fitting tribute to a place that still stands as a symbol of the Industrial Revolution and its effects on humanity.

**01.** There are now more than 6 kilometres (3.7 miles) of paths for visitors to follow through Völklingen Ironworks **02**. An average of 256 monorail cars were used to supply the blast furnaces with raw materials **03.** Enormous structures were built to house the operations of the ironworks

# Wieliczka Salt Mine

## *Poland* (Inscribed 1978)

Down and down, around and around, curiouser and curiouser. As you explore the warren of Poland's Wieliczka Salt Mine, it feels as though you're continually going deeper, getting more disoriented, chamber after chamber. It's easy to lose your sense of everything but wonder – after all, there are more than 245 kilometres (152 miles) of tunnels down here that have been excavated since the 13th century. The first shaft down into the mine was struck about 700 years ago and it was in use until 1996, by which time there were 26 shafts, the mine going 327 metres (1072 feet) deep.

However, it's not the scale of Wieliczka Salt Mine that will be the most striking feature when you visit – most tours stick to a standard 2.5 kilometre (1.5 mile) trail – it's the decorations that will dazzle. Over the years, the miners spent so much time underground that they turned it into their own mini-city. They carved halls and churches, dining rooms

01

and dormitories. Little nooks became chapels covered with religious iconography.

During its operation, the mine made Polish kings, conquering empires, and elected governments very wealthy – salt was a valuable commodity for preserving food and Wieliczka was one of the most important in Europe. But the miners saw a different value, and they carved beautiful ornate statues out of the rock salt, decorating older excavations as they went deeper. One of the most notable artworks is relatively recent, from 1973, and is a likeness of astronomer Nicolaus Copernicus to commemorate his visit to the mine in 1493.

The most dazzling room is St Kinga's Chapel, as large as many above-ground churches, it's 54 metres long (177 feet), 18 metres wide (59 feet), and 12 metres high (39 feet). The entire room is made from salt – the floor carved in a uniform salt mass, dozens of statues on the walls, the altar a piece of carved salt, even

the glittering chandeliers are made from salt crystals. It took three men almost 70 years to create, between 1896 and 1964, yet it feels hauntingly timeless, beautiful and radiant in a dark and dangerous underground realm.

St Kinga's Chapel may be the most impressive, but there are 2350 chambers in Wieliczka Salt Mine. My guide told me that, at the pace of her tours, it would take more than seven weeks to visit all of them. Thankfully the mandatory tour includes a good selection of older and modern rooms, plus the eerie underground lake with an illuminated wooden path, where visitors could once do boat tours. Without someone leading, you might never find some of these rooms ... or the way out!

**01.** St Kinga's Chapel, which took almost 70 years to carve **02.** Visitors are led on guided tours through just a fraction of the mine's tunnels **03.** A statue of Nicolaus Copernicus, carved from salt in 1973

# Jodrell Bank Observatory

## *United Kingdom* (Inscribed 2019)

We may be talking about World Heritage Sites, but what about Galaxy Heritage Sites, or Universe Heritage Sites? Perhaps one day we will be living amongst the other stars – and Jodrell Bank Observatory will have played a part in that.

Established in 1945, it was one of the first radio astronomy observatories in the world, peering further than we can see with our eyes through a telescope, deep into the universe, from where invisible signals are beamed to paint a picture of the most outer of spaces. The Jodrell Bank Observatory has played a key role in our understanding of the universe, its astronomers like pioneers exploring new lands.

Radio telescopes are quite remarkable-looking contraptions (and I say that as someone who grew up around them, with astrophysicists as parents). There are several at Jodrell Bank Observatory, but one dominates the site: the Lovell Telescope. Operational from 1957, it was the largest of its era, an enormous white dish with a diameter of 76 metres (249 feet), supported on a huge metal frame with 50-metre-high (164-feet) supporting legs on two sides. The whole telescope can rotate on circular railway tracks and it has mechanisms that can tilt the dish all the way to the horizon, opening up the entire sky.

Radio astronomy was still in its early stages when the Lovell Telescope was built, so it was at the forefront of the Space Age. One of its first successes was tracking the carrier rocket for Sputnik 1, the world's first satellite launched into space. The idea of gazing so far beyond our galaxy inspired ordinary people, and the first visitor centre was built here in 1966. It was replaced with the more modern Discovery Centre in 2011.

The overall layout of Jodrell Bank Observatory hasn't changed since the mid-1960s and the Lovell Telescope continues to scan through space, continually adding to our knowledge of the universe. Even today, it is still the third-largest steerable radio telescope (after the Green Bank Telescope in the United States of America and Effelsberg Telescope in Germany). The site has discovered so much about space, including things we didn't even know we should be looking for. How many other secrets of the cosmos will be revealed here?

# The Jodrell Bank Observatory has played a key role in our understanding of the universe, its astronomers like pioneers exploring new lands.

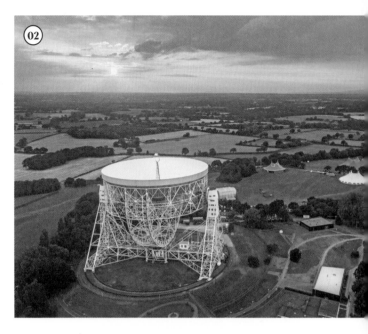

**01.** The Jodrell Bank Observatory was founded in 1945, making it one of the first of its kind in the world **02.** The dish of the main Lovell Telescope has a diameter of 76 metres (249 feet) **03.** The Lovell Telescope tilts and rotates on railway tracks so it can point at every part of the sky

# Tomioka Silk Mill

## *Japan* (Inscribed 2014)

On either side of the aisle running down the centre of Tomioka Silk Mill's main building is a row of old machines with silent green wheels, spotless and covered in plastic sheets for protection. Brought here from France at the end of the 19th century, the machines were part of the first major industrialisation of Japan, a key step in its evolution into a modern global nation.

After a long period of isolation, Japan opened the Port of Yokohama to the world in 1859, and raw silk made up about 65 per cent of the

exports. Just a decade later, under Emperor Meiji, Japan wanted to capitalise on this, so imported the cocoon reeling machines and leading experts from France. In partnership, they built Tomioka Silk Mill, with structures purpose-built for every stage of the production process. (The buildings themselves are a fusion of French construction methods and Japanese design styles.)

Preparing to open the new silk mill in 1872, the Japanese Government tried to recruit young women as workers but was surprised that,

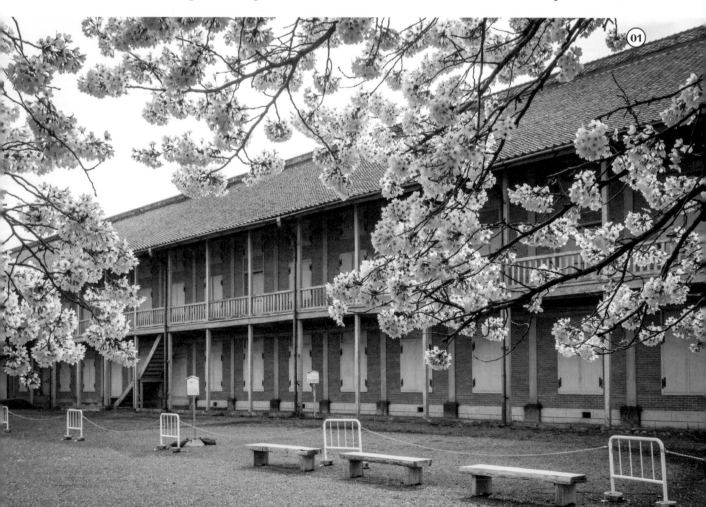

despite good pay and conditions, very few were applying. It turned out the women were scared of the French technical advisers because they thought they drank human blood. Of course, it was just red wine that had sparked the rumours! In the end, Tomioka Silk Mill was actually one of the country's first initiatives to give women a more active role in society, also teaching them how to read, write, and use an abacus – skills that helped them get more senior roles elsewhere. However, this isn't mentioned in the official World Heritage Site listing – except for a passing reference to the 'women's dormitories' – a good example of the gender bias that UNESCO acknowledges is a problem in its system (*see* p. 202).

The young women were employed here for their small hands, which could delicately manipulate the cocoons of silk onto reels and extract the threads from the machines in the main building. Next to the equipment, you can

still see the five large boilers used to soften the cocoons beforehand. Other buildings in the central complex were used to store cocoons and package the silk. A bit further away were staff quarters and dormitories for the workers. Tomioka Silk Mill feels today like the museum it is, and it has been well preserved since it finished operation in 1987.

The Japanese authorities knew how important it was for the industrialisation of their silk industry to be successful, so they developed other aspects that are also part of the World Heritage Site. About 30 kilometres (18.6 miles) away is a farm used to grow mulberry trees to feed the silk worms, and buildings for the eggs and larvae. About 12 kilometres (7.4 miles) away is a school that was used to pass on knowledge about the silk worm industry, a sector that still exists but has been eclipsed by an enormous economy that Tomioka helped build.

**01.** The architecture of the Tomioka Silk Mill was inspired by Japanese styles but used French construction methods **02.** Cocoons were softened in boiling water before being placed in the machines **03.** The reeling machines brought from France in the 19th century are now protected by plastic sheets

# Gender bias in World Heritage

Take a look at the list of World Heritage Sites in this chapter, and you will see that almost all of them are industries dominated by men. In fact, across the whole World Heritage List, in every instance a site has been named in honour of a particular person, that person is male. It's an obvious bias – and it's not the only one. The list also has a bias towards wealthy countries, towards a more European idea of what is 'valuable', and towards cultures that fit into a concept of society that we understand today. While much of this is subconscious, it perpetuates discriminatory views of how to define heritage.

Not every World Heritage Site is focused purely on men, though. There is, for example, the **Flemish Béguinages** in Belgium, which were enclosed communities founded by and for women in the 13th century; and the rock art at **Chongoni** in Malawi, which is related to female ceremonies and rituals. There is also the **Cascades Female Factory** in Hobart, Australia, that housed women convicts and kept them separate from the colony; and the French wine-producing region of **Champagne**, where the World Heritage Site listing specifically makes mention of women playing a special role in the product's evolution.

While UNESCO is, very diplomatically, not critical of any particular site or country, it has highlighted that there is often a power imbalance in who is choosing World Heritage Sites. If they are usually male, and usually from dominant or colonising cultures, there can be an unconscious bias towards a cultural history seen through a particular lens. Even evaluations in 2005 and 2010 of the independent advisers that assess World Heritage Sites for UNESCO found only about 20 per cent were women.

In recent years, UNESCO has tried to redress gender bias, as well as the geographic imbalance, by offering more assistance to countries that have struggled with the long bureaucratic process required to successfully get a site listed, a major factor in why some countries have a lot and some have very little. (About 40 per cent of World Heritage Sites are in just ten countries!) Ultimately, though, it's the people in each country making decisions about nominations who will play the biggest role.

At least the issues of bias are now being discussed openly and there are attempts to remedy the most egregious examples. But bureaucracy, like heritage, is a gradual process.

Chongoni, Malawi **Inset** Flemism Béguinage in Bruges, Belgium

# The Great Wall

## *China* (Inscribed 1987)

Of all the engineering marvels in history, perhaps none is quite as marvellous as the Great Wall of China. In basic terms, it is the world's largest human-made object. But there is nothing simple about this monument, which stretches for more than 20,000 kilometres (12,427 miles) across northern China, colossal lines of defence repelling invaders and propelling a nation to greatness.

The Great Wall is actually a series of walls, built at different times in different areas, depending on the exact threats. However, the most famous section was built by the Ming Dynasty between the 14th and 17th centuries. It covers 8850 kilometres (5500 miles), with about 70 per cent being actual wall and the rest consisting of trenches or natural barriers like rivers. The construction methods had come a long way since the first iteration of the Great Wall, which came in the 3rd century BCE, when emperor Qin Shi Huang connected older fortifications to create a continuous line made with bits of local stone and rammed earth. The wall was gradually extended and improved under successive leaders but it was generally neglected from the 5th century until the Ming revival.

What you see today when you visit the Great Wall is what was built by the Ming Dynasty, which restarted the massive construction project to defend against tribes from Mongolia. Along the thousands of kilometres of walls,

25,000 watchtowers and 15,000 outposts were built. When I walked a stretch of the wall at Mutianyu, some 75 kilometres (46.6 miles) north of Beijing, it felt like I was climbing every one of those watchtowers. The steep staircases up to them are arduous, requiring a firm grip to half support and half pull. But going through each tower is the only way to pass. The path at the top of the wall, several metres wide, was designed for troops or couriers to move quickly along the mountainous terrain. You need to take it slowly now, though – much of it hasn't

been restored (although sections like Mutianya and Badaling, designated as tourist areas, are much better than most of the fortification line).

The popular myth that the Great Wall of China can be seen from space is unfortunately false, but it really doesn't matter. You wouldn't be able to appreciate it from up there. It's here, clambering up the steps to a watchtower, the yellow brick path leading your eye over hills to the horizon, dotted with more towers, that you can really appreciate its scale. It may be the length that sounds the most impressive but, for a Mongol trying to invade, just the section right in front of them would have imposing enough.

**01.** The Great Wall of China stretches for more than 20,000 kilometres (12,400 miles) across northern China **02.** Looking out across a stretch of the wall from one of the watchtowers **03.** Across the length of the entire wall, there are about 25,000 towers

# Fray Bentos Complex

*Uruguay* (Inscribed 2015)

A dilapidated wooden dock juts out from the coastline into the Uruguay River, which forms the border with Argentina, about 1.5 kilometres (0.9 miles) across the water. Spreading inland from the dock is the large industrial complex of Fray Bentos, rows of brick buildings with saw-tooth roofs of corrugated iron. For more than a century, the site was used for processing meat that was sent across the globe – sustaining armies during World Wars, becoming a household name for many families, and even feeding young British royalty. When Prince Charles visited Uruguay in 1999, he remarked, 'I remember eating corned beef until it came out of my ears'.

A meat salting works was established on the site in 1859 and, from 1865, the Liebig Extract of Meat Company began exporting meat extract and corned beef to the European market. Renamed as the Anglo Meatpacking Plant from 1924, it began to also export frozen meat.

01

The company reached its peak during World War II and in the post-war period, because the preserved meat was so convenient. In 1943 alone, more than 16 million cans of corned beef were sent from Fray Bentos to Europe.

The industrial complex you find today has been protected by the Uruguayan Government since operations stopped here in 1979, but the minor damage that comes with time hasn't been repaired – paneless windows, broken gates, and metal sheets missing from the roofs of walkways, for instance. The production line is clear, though, with buildings even connected by internal roads, conveyor lines, and aerial tunnels. Visually it makes sense for visitors, beginning at the wide green pastures where cows would graze, through holding pens, slaughter yards, processing sheds, and through to the enormous concrete building used for cold storage next to the river where boats would be loaded.

It's hard to think about what actually took place in some of these buildings and not wince a little, but unfortunately that was the reality of the mass production of animal products. However, from a scientific and technological perspective, the meat extraction and packaging methods were revolutionary and changed dietary habits around the world. You may even still find a steak and kidney pie with the Fray Bentos label at your local supermarket.

**01.** The Fray Bentos complex is situated on the Uruguay River, offering easy access for transport ships **02.** Parts of the industrial complex had fallen into disrepair, although it now has heritage protection **03.** Fray Bentos products are still for sale in many supermarkets around the world

# Plantin-Moretus House and Workshops

*Belgium* (Inscribed 2005)

On the western side of Vrijdagmarkt, one of the market squares in the Belgian city of Antwerp, the simple façade of the Plantin-Moretus Museum understates the significance of what lies beyond. This building was the home and workshop of one of the greatest printer-publishers in history, Christophe Plantin. From 1555, he printed books including the world's first atlas, the first Dutch dictionary, and his masterpiece – an eight-part Bible in five languages. During his 34-year career, Plantin produced 1887 major publications, with at least 1000 copies of each. At the centre of the spread of human knowledge, his effect on Western civilisation was immense.

When Plantin died in 1589, he left the printing business to his son-in-law, Jan Moretus, and it stayed in the family for another three centuries until it was sold to the Belgian Government in 1867 to become the museum you find today. It houses the two oldest printing presses in the world, from around 1600, and six others from the 17th and 18th centuries that still work. The smell of ink no longer hangs heavy in the air but you can almost sense it as you walk through the history.

A large collection of the books produced here – as well as other notable historic works – are on display at the Great Library that Plantin

**01.** There are thousands of books in the Great Library, which was designed in a humanist style **02.** By printing at least a thousand copies of each book, the text was able to be widely disseminated **03.** The museum has eight printing presses on display, two of them about 400 years old

founded with a humanist style, busts and paintings decorating the antique room. Elsewhere in the complex is the small shop where books were sold from about 1700, and the residential wing, lavishly adorned to reflect the success of the business. The museum also has an impressive art collection, including dozens of portraits that Plantin's grandson, Balthasar I Moretus, commissioned from his childhood friend, Peter Paul Rubens.

These days, we take easy access to information for granted, but its introduction centuries ago changed the world. Johannes Gutenberg may get the credit for the invention of the mechanical printing press in the mid-15th century, but it's those who stood on his shoulders who reached the highest.

During his 34-year career, Plantin produced 1887 major publications, with at least 1000 copies of each. At the centre of the spread of human knowledge, his effect on Western civilisation was immense.

# Sewell Mining Town

*Chile* (Inscribed 2006)

Just as the rivers flow down from the Andes, so does the wealth of Chile. For here, high in the mountainous border region, are the natural resources which have made the country one of the most stable economies in South America. Chile has about 30 per cent of the world's copper resources and the mining of it still accounts for about 10 per cent of the country's GDP. Over the years, many mines have come and gone, leaving husks amongst the peaks, and the most famous of these is the old mining town of Sewell that clings to a mountainside.

Built in 1904 at what was to become the world's largest underground copper mine,

El Teniente, Sewell was in continuous use for decades, until workers were moved to the nearby city of Rancagua in the 1970s. But because mining operations continued on the site, the abandoned buildings were maintained somewhat, leaving us with a snapshot of this industrial community.

At its peak, Sewell had a population of about 15,000 people, creating a bustling and lively community for workers and their families, 2300 metres (7545 feet) above sea level. The residents may have left but the vibrancy has remained, shining through the bright colours that the buildings were painted, rich greens, yellows, reds, and blues. They stand out in stark contrast to the desolate rocky landscape with no trace of vegetation. The buildings were constructed up the sheer slope of the mountain – so steep that it was impossible for vehicles to move around it – so Sewell was accessed by an enormous central staircase leading up from the train station, and then a convoluted network of steps and pathways connecting various areas.

As I climbed the steps and followed the paths, I was struck by the quiet and emptiness – not a surprise, but still unsettling, especially when there are still flowers blooming in pots, curtains half-pulled in windows, and playground equipment that looks like it was just used. The paint may be peeling and the railings may be rusting, but parts of the town have a ghost-like appearance, caught in a dimension between the past and the present. There are the five-storey buildings that provided

accommodation – families had their own space but single workers shared dormitories with bunk beds; there's the hospital, church, theatre, and bowling alley; and surrounding it all is the industrial complex where ore and minerals from the mine were ground and concentrated in a consistent cacophony.

Most of the noise at Sewell Mining Town now comes from the fiercely cold winds that slam into the mountain, but there is still a little activity from workers passing through, because the mine is still operational. The abandoned buildings here are a testament to that wealth ... and the workers who made it possible.

01. Many workers lived in shared dormitories within apartment blocks 02. With no roads, residents used staircases and pathways to get around the town 03. It's an eerie feeling in the town, which has been preserved well since it was abandoned

The colourful Sewell Mining Town hugs the side of a steep mountain

# Going underground

Sometimes, to explore history you need to do more than just scratch the surface. There are more than a dozen World Heritage Sites that protect former mines, and going underground is a fascinating way to get a deeper look at the labour that enriched empires and has powered the world's industrial and technological revolutions.

In Bolivia, the silver mine known as **Cerro Rico** (Rich Mountain) at the city of Potosí is still in use, but nothing like at its zenith in the 16th century when it was regarded as the world's largest industrial complex. It was mined by the Spanish colonial power and, until the 18th century when production eased, it supplied about 80 per cent of the silver in the world.

In the period that followed, **Guanajuato** in Mexico became the world's leading silver-extraction centre and is known for a 600-metre-deep (1968-foot) mineshaft known as Boca del Infierno (Mouth of Hell). You can visit several of the old mines but the colourful city is also a highlight.

At **Ouro Preto** in Brazil, the beautiful Baroque city is the focus, built with the wealth from the gold mines used by Portuguese colonialists between the 17th and 19th centuries.

During the Industrial Revolution, the Dutch colonial government developed **Ombilin** coal mine in an inaccessible region of Sumatra in Indonesia that was in use in the late 19th and early 20th centuries. As well as the mining tunnels, the UNESCO site has protected the company town built on the surface and the rail network to the coast.

Across Europe, there are quite a few mines that have been used in different historical periods. Gold, silver, and other metals were extracted in **Banská Štiavnica** in Slovakia from the 13th century and a wealthy city was created around it, including Europe's first mining academy. An enormous pit at **Falun** in Sweden marks an extensive copper mining industry from the 13th until the late 20th century. And **Røros** in Norway still has thousands of small wooden houses built as part of the copper mining that took place here from the 17th century until 1977, leaving a permanent cultural mark on the landscape.

Although all of these mines have been protected as a testament to the industries that built the modern world, it's interesting to note that UNESCO has identified the current mining industry as the seventh biggest threat to the conservation of World Heritage Sites (particularly natural ones in Africa).

Røros, Norway **Inset** Cerro Rico, Bolivia

# Stari Grad Plain

## *Croatia* (Inscribed 2008)

With so much technological change over the generations, it's quite remarkable to find an industry that still operates the way it did 2400 years ago. But on the farmland of the Stari Grad Plain on the Croatian island of Hvar, agriculture continues as it has since it was founded. Other than the occasional sound of a car from the nearby roads, today on the plain could almost be the 4th century BCE, when the Ionian Greeks arrived and established their innovative farming practice.

These new settlers organised the plain into geometric plots that were separated with boundaries of dry-stone wall. They were then connected to tanks and gutters that collected rainwater, which was distributed as needed. An ingenuous system, it enabled the farmers to grow grapes, olives, and vegetables sustainably for the whole community. In the centuries to come, this system spread across Europe.

As I cycled along a dirt path between the fields, ancient walls on either side, I could see olive trees swaying in the slight breeze, vineyards creating lush green lines amongst the dirt, and a tonal patchwork of crops spreading out for kilometres. There's not much traffic on Hvar and most vehicles use the sealed road around the outside of the Stari Grad Plain, so the

01

rustic tracks through it are quiet with cyclists, walkers, and just the occasional farmer with a motorbike or truck. The agricultural plots cover an area about 5 kilometres long (3.1 miles) and 2 kilometres wide (1.2 miles) and, although it may seem odd for tourists to visit farmland, passing through is a convenient way to get between the historic coastal towns of Stari Grad, Vrboska, and Jelsa, each a delightful little community of Renaissance buildings set around a small port.

Look closer and you'll find other reasons to visit the Stari Grad Plain itself. Small chapels built at the edge of the fields between the 15th and 19th centuries offer a peek at the daily life of farmers; and some of the producers now offer agritourism, where you can taste the wine and meals cooked with the food grown in these ancient plots.

# Other than the occasional sound of a car from the nearby roads, today on the plain could almost be the 4th century BCE

**01.** The small Chapel of Our Lady (Gospojica) was built on the plain in the late 16th century **02.** Dry walls made of stone were used to separate the plots of land **03.** Stari Grad Plain is still used today by local farmers to grow crops

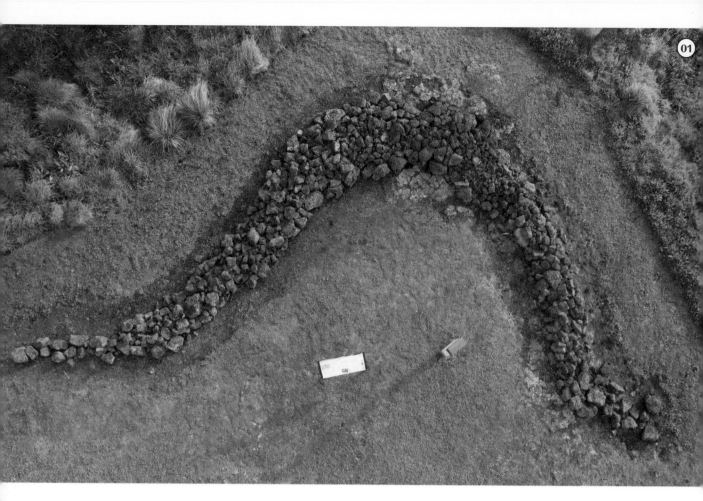

# Budj Bim

## *Australia* (Inscribed 2019)

About 37,000 years ago, the Gunditjmara people saw the Budj Bim volcano erupt. Budj Bim was an ancestral being who was, as torrents of lava streamed down for more than 50 kilometres (31 miles), consciously creating a new landscape. This changed earth would be more than just a different visual environment – the grooves in the ground formed by the lava flows would be instrumental in the extensive aquaculture system the Gunditjmara developed here, one of the oldest and finest examples of ancient engineering. When Australia nominated Budj Bim as a World Heritage Site, the documentation included a quote from Gunditjmara Elder, Aunty Eileen Alberts, who explained the significance of the land. 'In the Dreaming, the Ancestral Creators gave the Gunditjmara people the resources to live a settled lifestyle. They diverted the waterways, and gave us the stones and rocks to help us build the aquaculture system. They gave us the wetlands where the reeds grew so that we could make the eel baskets, and they gave us the food-enriched landscape for us to survive.'

The earliest evidence that can still be seen of the aquaculture is about 6600 years old. It was an ingenious system, where the Gunditjmara modified channels to divert waterways into holding ponds, meaning kooyang (short-finned eels) could be kept alive and then eaten at the best times. The kooyang grew fat and were harvested with woven baskets that were held by weirs built from volcanic rocks and wood lattice structures. In some areas, the system was quite complex, such as around Tyrendarra, where there is a series of 18 interconnected stone wall dams and seven excavated channels.

For six millennia, the farming practices here provided the Gunditjmara with a cultural and economic base, to harvest eels and smoke them for food and trade. Their traditional home includes the landscapes that you will still find today when you visit Budj Bim National Park and the other protected areas that cover the aquaculture system. There's the rugged stone country around the area where the volcano erupted (now just 178 metres/ 584 feet high), woodlands full of white gums and koalas snoozing in their branches, down to the swampy wetlands with their watery depressions that you can imagine filled with trapped kooyang.

And for thousands of years the stories of its creation have been passed down through countless generations of Gunditjmara families, telling of a 'deep time', an idea that their Country was brought to life by beings which were sometimes human, sometimes animal, and sometimes neither. But what the Gunditjmara did with this land is the most incredible part of the story, and that we can still see it 6600 years later is just as remarkable.

01. The aquaculture system trapped kooyang within the wetlands 02. Visitors can take tours of Budj Bim with local Indigenous guides 03. Budj Bim National Park has a variety of different ecosystems

# History's great empires

From mighty Rome to the mysterious Maya, every empire that rises ultimately falls with the natural ebb and flow of history. But even when these epic civilisations recede, they leave behind a legacy that makes a permanent mark on the world, which can often be seen at a UNESCO World Heritage Site.

Sometimes it is cultural, like the philosophy of Ancient Greece still underpinning our ideals today and perhaps best represented by the Acropolis (*see* p. 226); or political, such as the Byzantine and Ottoman Empires bridging two powerful continents, and still shaping modern Istanbul (*see* p. 234). But almost always it's physical – the Giza Pyramids of Ancient Egypt (*see* p. 222), the Incan citadel of Machu Picchu (*see* p. 228), the Silk Road city of Samarkand (*see* p. 232), and the royal city of Ayutthaya (*see* p. 244).

It's in the ancient imperial capitals, hulking temples, ornate tombs, and other iconic monuments that we find these civilisations. How incredible it would have been to see them at their peak, full of pomp and people. At least through our travels to their remnants and ruins, we gain a view into the history-shaping empires of the world.

# The Giza Pyramids

## *Egypt* (Inscribed 1979)

It doesn't matter how many times you've heard stories or seen photos of the Egyptian pyramids, standing there, looking up at the towering ancient monuments, their sheer scale will still shock you.

The largest of the Giza Pyramids, known as the Pyramid of Khufu or the Great Pyramid, was built between 2551–2528 BCE and is thought to have been the tallest structure in the world for about 3800 years (finally overtaken by the Lincoln Cathedral in England in 1311). It is 150 metres high (492 feet), and was constructed with about 2.3 million stone blocks, the lightest being about 2 tonnes. These blocks would once have been covered by a surface of polished limestone, now collapsed or removed, so when you get close you can now make out their individual shapes, some as tall as people, some just small enough to clamber up.

The shape of the pyramids was not chosen simply for its stability. It also represents rays of sunlight, connecting the pharaohs to the sun god, Amun Ra, because that's how the people saw their rulers – as a representative on earth for the deities. It is surely one of the ways that tens of thousands of people were convinced to help with the mammoth construction projects. (Although it's a common belief the pyramids were built by slaves, most historians now agree it was done by paid labourers who thought it would improve their afterlife.)

There are three main pyramids at Giza, thought to be the tombs for three generations of kings

01

**01.** The Sphinx in front of the Pyramid of Khafre **02.** Some of the polished limestone that once covered the structures remains at the top of the Pyramid of Khafre **03.** The lightest of the blocks used to build the Great Pyramid weigh about 2 tonnes

from Khufu to his son Khafre and grandson Menkaure. Although they were pharaohs in the very early years of Ancient Egypt, around 2500 BCE, their resting places, rising so dramatically from the yellow desert with modern Cairo expanding to their doorstep, have become symbols of the whole empire.

They are not just breathtaking, but they also exude a sense of mystery. What else might be hidden deep beneath those stones, along secret passages and in ancient treasure chambers? In 2017, a scan of the Great Pyramid found an unexplained and inaccessible void in the structure.

There is even still a mystery about the Sphinx, the mythical human-headed lion that guards the causeway to the second-largest pyramid, the Pyramid of Khafre. Many experts believe there was once a second sphinx that

stood beside it, maybe now buried in the sand somewhere on the site, perhaps right beneath the feet of the throngs of tourists who come every day to see these great monuments.

As Ancient Egypt continued to flourish after the early dynasties, there was a good reason that the Ancient Egyptians stopped building pyramids for their dead rulers. For grave robbers, they were a huge marker for where they could find the treasures buried with a pharaoh for their afterlife. Instead, the Egyptians began to place the sarcophagi into underground tombs in necropolises like the Valley of the Kings, about 500 kilometres (311 miles) south (and part of another World Heritage Site, *see* p. 116). But these ancient burial grounds create even more exciting potential for new mysteries to be revealed, as Howard Carter proved with the discovery in 1922 of the Tomb of Tutankhamun.

# Rome

### *Italy* (Inscribed 1980)

The Roman Empire was one of the largest in history, stretching across most of Europe and into North Africa and Asia. From Hadrian's Wall in Britain, to an outpost at Volubilis in Morocco, through the Balkans with the Palace of Galerius in Serbia, into Jordan to the incredible city of Jerash, and down into Egypt. Even the most casual of travellers will inevitably trip over some Roman ruins or discover some mosaics.

At the heart of it all was Rome itself, the bustling nerve centre that controlled the empire. From here, emperors sent soldiers to conquer, engineers to build, collectors to tax. What made Rome so powerful was not simply its military, but the way it integrated people across the continent into a system of daily life that was hard to escape. (And we think globalisation is a modern thing!)

It's perhaps best represented by the Roman Forum, a sprawling site that still exists today, albeit in a state of ruin. It was from here that the empire was governed, where the population would gather to hear orations, take part in processions, watch trials and vote in elections. But it was about more than politics. It also served as an enormous market, attracting tens of thousands of visitors, with stalls, shops and taverns. It was the world's greatest meeting place.

Visiting today, walking along the ancient avenues, you can see the shells of the magnificent buildings that would have once filled the Forum – massive temples and basilicas, palaces and arches. Columns rise up towards the sky, wide marble avenues streak across the ground, monumental foundations trace the shape of the mighty civic centre. You can even see some of the Curia Julia, the red-brick senate house built by Julius Caesar where philosophical battles took place.

It was next door, at the Colosseum, where the real battles took place. Constructed between 72–80 CE by three consecutive emperors of the Flavian dynasty (hence its original name: the Flavian Amphitheatre), it was the largest ancient amphitheatre ever built. More than 50,000 people could fill the stands, their roars echoing around the large stone oval. Perhaps they would be supporting a

gladiator, perhaps they would be shouting for someone's death. You can almost imagine Russell Crowe standing down there, looking up at the spectators, shouting back, 'Are you not entertained?'

It would be a fair thing to ask, because the Colosseum was primarily used for wholesome entertainment like dramas, re-enactments of famous historical events, and elaborate productions with the arena full of animals and trees. A sophisticated system under the floor allowed for complex staging to turn a show into a spectacle.

And, like almost everything else in the Roman Empire, it was all about power, the likes of which the world has rarely seen. It may have been created in the Forum but it was on full display in the Colosseum.

**01.** The Roman Forum, the centre of civic life in Ancient Rome **02.** The floor of the Colosseum's arena has been removed, so visitors can see some of the staging system below **03.** From left to right, the Arch of Septimius Severus, the Santi Luca e Martina church, and the Curia Julia

# The Acropolis of Athens

*Greece* (Inscribed 1987)

We still owe a lot to the Ancient Greeks. Across the world, you can see their legacy in systems of government, philosophical principles, mathematical equations, and even theatrical styles (which is no tragedy). While Ancient Greece didn't conquer and expand over great tracts of land like the Romans, it was one of the most influential periods in history, often described as the 'Cradle of Western Civilisation'.

The most complete physical legacy remaining from that era is the Acropolis of Athens, the

complex of ancient buildings on a rocky outcrop in the centre of the Greek capital. The hill of the Acropolis dominates the landscape of Athens, an enormous beacon that can be seen across the centre of the city, rising up from the otherwise flat urbanity. Here, the Ancient Greeks built temples to several gods, primarily Athena, the patron saint of the city.

Climbing up the steep slippery stone stairs to the top of the hill, you first pass through the majestic gateway known as the Propylaea, a

01

marble structure supported by Doric columns that was both ceremonial and practical, to control who could enter. Once on the flat top, with Athens stretching out below in every direction, the first temple visitors often spot is the Erechtheum, with the impressive Porch of the Maidens, where the six columns are detailed sculptures of women in flowing dresses.

But, of course, the most important – and by far the largest – temple on the Acropolis is the Parthenon, dedicated to Athena but worshipped today as a symbol of Ancient Greece and its legacy. Built in the 5th century BCE, it's a massive marble structure about 70 metres long (230 feet) and 30 metres wide (98 feet), with 46 thick fluted columns around the exterior, 17 on each side and eight at each end.

While the Parthenon was nominally a temple, many historians believe it also acted as a treasury for Athens and was about projecting the wealth of the state as much as the depth of its faith. There's certainly no debate that

one of the building's main treasures was the 160-metre-long (525-foot) carved marble frieze that adorned the top of an interior wall of the temple, depicting a festival's procession to the Acropolis. It's the subject of huge controversy, because much of it was taken by Scottish diplomat Lord Elgin in the early 1800s and is still on display in the British Museum. Now known as the Elgin Marbles, Greece has been demanding for decades they be returned, and has purpose-built empty spaces for them in the large modern Acropolis Museum, opened in 2009. However, the British Museum claims more people will be able to appreciate them in London, and its website has a statement from the museum's trustees saying, 'they're a part of the world's shared heritage and transcend political boundaries'. It's undoubtedly not the way Ancient Greece would have imagined its culture spreading across the world.

---

**01.** The view through the Acropolis out to the city of Athens below **02.** The Parthenon was built with 46 thick columns around its exterior **03.** Although the Acropolis is in ruins, you'll still find parts of many of the original buildings

# Machu Picchu

## *Peru* (Inscribed 1983)

When the Spanish conquistadors invaded Peru in the 16th century, they never made it as far as Machu Picchu. The great Incan city, high in the mountains, remained hidden from them and it wasn't until hundreds of years later, when American historian Hiram Bingham 'discovered' it in 1911, that it was revealed to the rest of the world for the first time.

When I visited Machu Picchu, it was the sun that revealed the city to me, slowly rising into the dawn and spreading an orange glow across the site. The ruins of the old stone buildings hug one mountaintop, while the layout of the others around the valley create the impression that Machu Picchu is an island floating in a lake of air, with the shoreline produced by peaks circling even higher around it.

This is presumably why the Incas chose this site to build their city, with one theory that the mountains form a map for significant stellar bodies. Although nobody is completely certain what Machu Picchu was, the most common explanations are that it was either a royal retreat for the Incan emperor, or it was a sacred citadel for worship and religious administration. Perhaps it was a combination, or maybe it was something completely different. The mystery just adds to the magic.

What we do know is there are about 200 buildings at Machu Picchu, including temples and palaces. It operated like a small self-contained city, with houses for production of goods, fields for farming, a gaol, and a cemetery. Some of the structures were packed tightly together, like rows of terrace houses, while others flowed more organically down the actual terraces built into the side of the mountain. With a beautiful and almost unworldly blending between the buildings and the environment, it's sometimes unclear where the unnatural ends and the natural begins.

A certain amount of imagination is needed to create an impression of how the city would've looked – gold and silver hanging everywhere, great costumes for the high priests, a vibrant industrial sector, and messengers running in and out through the main gates and across mountains to relay messages to other outposts along the great Incan road system.

The system of roads that the Incas built across the Andes stretches over six modern-day countries and is a World Heritage Site in itself. Perhaps the most famous part of it is the Inca Trail, the four-day hike along original stone pathways and stairs that ends at the Sun Gate,

the ceremonial entrance to Machu Picchu. For hikers who are willing to rise early on the final morning, walking through the gate as the first rays hit the city may feel like discovering this wonder for the first time. But things have come a long way since the time of the Incas – many visitors now get one of the trains from Cusco to the base of the site and catch a bus to the top.

**01.** The peak of Huayna Picchu rises up at the end of the Incan city **02.** Terraces were built into the mountainside of Machu Picchu for agriculture **03.** The urban layout with houses and ceremonial buildings is still clear

# Calakmul

## *Mexico* (Inscribed 2002)

Visiting the ancient Mayan site of Calakmul is perhaps the closest an average tourist can come to the feeling of discovering a lost city. Deep in the Mexican jungle, near the border with Guatemala, Calakmul is rarely visited, even though it was once one of the civilisation's largest metropolises. On the day I went, there were fewer than 10 other people across the whole site, which made it even scarier when a howler monkey let out a tiger-like roar and it echoed around the ancient temples.

Many people associate the Maya with cities like Chichén Itzá or Uxmal (both of which are also World Heritage Sites), but they came much later in the empire's history. Calakmul was founded around 600 BCE and reached its zenith in the 6th century CE, when it had a population of about 50,000 people. It would've been one of the region's superpowers, along with its great rival Tikal (*see* p. 34), just 100 kilometres (62 miles) away in Guatemala. The two metropolises were connected by trade and conflict, their relationship oscillating between friend and foe, depending on the mood of the leaders.

The infrastructure of Calakmul, known as the Snake Kingdom because of its serpentine

01

**01.** Structure 1 is the second-largest pyramid at the site, at just under 50 metres (164 feet) **02.** The jungle has encroached on the temples and pyramids within the city of Calakmul **03.** Visitors to Calakmul will find the site almost empty of other people

emblem, reflected its powerful status, with enormous pyramids and temples across the city. The largest (which is rather dully just named Structure 2) is almost 50 metres high (164 feet). It's one of the tallest Mayan buildings in the world and climbing up its steep steps, through the canopy of trees, gives you a panoramic vista across the jungle.

Throughout the site are also palaces, sporting arenas, ceremonial courts, and residential complexes. You can walk through the layouts of the houses and realise that they are not too dissimilar to modern designs, with bedrooms off central living areas. Now, though, there are trees growing out of walls – a fitting vision because the jungle became the main resident here from about 900 CE when Calakmul was abandoned and the Maya moved north.

# Calakmul is rarely visited, even though it was once one of the civilisation's largest metropolises.

# Samarkand

## *Uzbekistan* (Inscribed 2001)

The founder of the Timurid Empire in Central Asia, Timur (also known as Tamerlane) was one of the most 'successful' military leaders in history, establishing an enormous dominion. During the 14th century CE, he expanded his land west to east from Turkey to India, and south to north from Iran to Kazakhstan. Timur modelled his leadership on Genghis Khan, idolising him so much that he even married a descendant so they could be related.

As a conqueror, Timur was ruthless and it's estimated that his battles of conquest killed about 17 million people, about five per cent of the world's population at the time. Yet he also embraced art and architecture. Which is why he brought (probably kidnapped) the best artisans from across his empire to build his capital at Samarkand in Uzbekistan.

Samarkand became the most magnificent city in Central Asia, a jewel along the Silk Road. Many of the buildings that made it glitter still stand today. The most important complex is the Registan, a central square with large madrassas (Islamic schools) on three sides. These Islamic schools have striking façades intricately decorated with tiles of indigo and turquoise against warm golden bricks. Through the enormous arched entranceways are peaceful courtyards lined with small rooms for study.

My favourite part of Samarkand is the necropolis known as Shah-i-Zinda. Going through a nondescript gate, then taking a staircase up a hill, you arrive at an avenue of mausoleums covered in some of the best Islamic tile-work in the world, the green and blue mosaics leading you through to a shrine where Qusam, a cousin of the Prophet Muhammad, is said to be buried.

Another of the city's spectacular monuments is the Bibi-Khanym Mosque, with a 40-metre-high (131-foot) dome. It's said that Timur himself pushed the workers to build it as fast as possible, which may explain why it started to fall apart a few years after its construction in 1405 CE – the year that Timur died. It's an apt metaphor for the Timurid Empire, which also started to collapse a few years after Timur's death because it was too big to control.

Timur is buried at the spectacular tiled mausoleum built in his honour called Gur-i Amir ... and some say he still can control world events from here. In 1941, Joseph Stalin sent Soviet researchers to exhume the body to do scientific research and create a replica – but this may have unleashed a curse. Because, two days after the tomb of Timur was opened, Nazi Germany invaded the Soviet Union. When Stalin, who revered Timur as a warrior, heard the story, he demanded the body be returned. Not long after, the Soviets won the Battle of Stalingrad, a turning point in the war.

**01.** The necropolis of Shah-i-Zinda, with an avenue of mausoleums **02.** The open-air courtyard within one of the madrassas (Islamic schools) of the Registan **03.** A gate at the Registan, decorated with intricate tile-work

# Istanbul

## *Turkey* (Inscribed 1985)

There aren't many cities that were the capital for two distinct empires. There aren't many cities that straddle two continents. And there aren't many cities that have had three names. Istanbul has always been unique.

It's still a vibrant city today, with the smell of strong coffee from street cafes, bazaars bursting with colourful wares, and the constant squawking of seagulls. But it's the history that makes Istanbul – previously known as Constantinople, and Byzantium before that – such a compelling place. Even after the fall of the Roman Empire around the 5th century CE, it continued as the capital of the Byzantine Empire for almost a millennia, sowing its influence across much of Europe and North Africa. Then, after the city was conquered in the 15th century, it became the capital for the Ottoman Empire, creating a bridge across continents through which cultures were constantly exchanged.

The greatest monument in Istanbul from the Byzantine Empire is Hagia Sophia, built as a vast church in 537 CE, its interior covered with mosaics, supported by marble pillars on the sides, and with a soaring dome 55 metres high (180 feet). A brilliant piece of engineering that fused styles from east and west, it was the world's largest cathedral for about 1000 years.

01

When the Ottomans took control of the city in 1453, they not only turned Hagia Sophia into a mosque, they also built their own magnificent monument next to it – the Sultan Ahmed Mosque, also known as the Blue Mosque. It has five main domes, eight secondary domes, and six minarets, and inside, the coloured tiles that give the mosque its nickname cover the walls, interrupted only by the purples and yellows of thin stained-glass windows. Nearby is Topkapı Palace, the sprawling headquarters of the Ottoman sultans, built from the 15th century and now a museum with hundreds of rooms including a harem and a treasury.

At the top of a hill near the waterfront, the two grand places of worship stare across a crowded square at each other at the centre of the UNESCO-recognised Historic Areas of Istanbul, perhaps acknowledging the physical and ideological battles that have been fought on this land, and the melting pot of culture and religion they have created. In 2006, Pope Benedict XVI visited the Blue Mosque. It was only the second visit ever of a pope to a Muslim place of worship, but Istanbul's story as the centre of empires and bridge of continents makes it seem apt.

**01.** Inside Hagia Sophia, which was converted from a church to a mosque in 1453 CE **02.** The interior of the Sultan Ahmed Mosque (the Blue Mosque) covered in colourful tiles **03.** The Blue Mosque is one of the most recognisable icons of Istanbul

# Aksum

## *Ethiopia* (Inscribed 1980)

The Holy Grail is not the only biblical relic still sought by treasure hunters. Another that has never been discovered is the Ark of the Covenant, the gold-covered chest that's said to contain the two stone tablets carved with the Ten Commandments given to Moses by God.

Although there are many theories of where it could be, the most persistent is from the Ethiopian Orthodox Church, which claims that it possesses the Ark of the Covenant at the ancient city of Aksum. Legend says that it was given by King Solomon to his son, Menelik I, who became the first emperor of Ethiopia.

Irrespective of the truth of the story, Aksum itself was an extremely important city as the capital of the Aksumite Empire, a powerful force from the 1st until the 9th century CE. With its strategic position, it controlled most of the trade in the Red Sea, and was a significant commercial link between Africa, Arabia, and Ancient Rome.

The most distinctive part of the architecture of Aksum was the giant obelisks that were erected throughout the city. Some are plain and some are elaborately decorated with carvings

01

**01.** The obelisk on the ground would have been the tallest in the world, standing at 34 metres (111.5 feet) **02.** The Church of Saint Mary of Zion in Aksum is said to hold the Ark of the Covenant **03.** The ruins of a large mansion known as Dungur, or the Palace of the Queen of Sheba

of windows and doors, like thin ancient skyscrapers. Many are still standing and they're a highlight of a visit to the site, where most of the other structures from the time are in ruins.

One obelisk lying on the ground is 34 metres long (111.5 feet) and would have been the tallest in the world if it was erected (it's not clear if it fell during the process of putting it up or not). Another 24-metre-long (79-foot) obelisk, called the Obelisk of Aksum, that's 1700 years old, was taken to Rome in 1937 but, after a long diplomatic dispute, was finally returned and restored in 2008. It is now the defining icon of the Aksumite Empire.

Aksum itself was an extremely important city as the capital of the Aksumite Empire, a powerful force from the 1st until the 9th century CE.

# Persepolis

### *Iran* (Inscribed 1979)

There are some places in the world I particularly wish I could've seen at the pinnacle of their existence. Near the top of the list is Persepolis, one of the most glorious cities of the Ancient World, a rich complex of palaces and ceremonial buildings that blossomed at the heart of a great civilisation.

Persepolis was the ceremonial capital of the Achaemenid Empire, the first of the Persian Empires. It was the largest civilisation the world had seen at that point and, even in the 6th century BCE, had a sophisticated road system, postal service, and official language (Aramaic). Although the Achaemenid Empire had a huge army to control its vast lands, its leaders were considered rather liberal and cultured.

Not many people lived in Persepolis because it wasn't a capital city in the traditional sense. Rather, it was a showpiece for the kings to demonstrate their power, probably particularly to their subject states who had to present ceremonial gifts here.

The best artisans from across the empire were brought to Persepolis over several generations to build the lavish complex that stretched out over an enormous terrace, about 10 metres high (33 feet), with staircases leading up to it. There were palaces polished to look like marble, throne rooms, reception halls, and a treasury. Huge gateways with giant sculptures of winged bulls led to walls covered in sculpted friezes and courtyards lined with slender columns. Artworks depicted the leaders as conquerors.

Persepolis, one of the most glorious cities of the Ancient World, a rich complex of palaces and ceremonial buildings that blossomed at the heart of a great civilisation.

their guardian statues are enough to evoke a sense of grandeur, but they are just the beginning of hundreds of metres of avenues you can explore.

Perhaps Persepolis would have continued to thrive if it hadn't been for Alexander the Great, who plundered and burnt the city in 330 BCE. Although it continued to be inhabited for a while as part of the growing Macedonian Empire, its status declined quickly and the city of Istakhr, just 5 kilometres (3 miles) away, emerged as the next Persian capital. The Achaemenid rulers who created Persepolis were just the first of the great empires of Persia, which have been foundational in the heritage and culture of Iran and the region for more than two millennia until today.

We are lucky that most of the foundations of Persepolis still exist today. The city is in a state of ruin, but there's carved artwork on the walls in excellent condition, columns are still standing, the urban layout is clear and navigable. The monumental gateways with

**01.** The remaining columns of the Apadana Palace at Persepolis **02.** The buildings were covered in artwork, including carvings in the walls **03.** As a ceremonial capital, Persepolis was designed to elevate the status of the rulers

# Petra

## *Jordan* (Inscribed 1985)

Walking through the canyon known as the Siq that forms the entrance to Petra, you feel the intensity of the site. The narrow pathway winds its way between two steep red-rock walls, a beautiful natural formation with the promise of a spectacular manmade jewel at the end, getting closer at each turn, the anticipation building. And it doesn't disappoint, that moment you come out of the canyon and see for the first time the Treasury, one of the world's great wonders.

For a site that was hidden for centuries (until a Swiss explorer named Johann Burckhardt tricked the locals into showing him where it was in the early 1800s), Petra is now world famous, in a large part because it was used to film some of the *Indiana Jones and the Last Crusade* movie (1989). But because those scenes focused on the Treasury (a misnomer because it's actually a tomb), many people don't realise how much else there is to see in this vast site.

Petra was once an enormous city, existing from about the 3rd century BCE until the 5th century CE. It was the capital of the Nabataean Kingdom, a wealthy and powerful civilisation that was originally nomadic but

01

became an influential trader when it based itself at the crossroads of continents, right in the middle of land caravan routes that connected Africa, Asia, and Europe.

The Nabataean built Petra with their wealth, for comfort and protection, but also as an administrative base as their empire expanded. It had temples and palaces, towers and a theatre. At its apogee, there were homes for about 20,000 people. The most recognisable remains today are the tombs with elegant façades cut into the rock-faces.

One of the most impressive tombs is known as the Monastery and is accessible by hiking up into the hills, where it's hidden from view from the main part of the city. It is 50 metres wide (164 feet), two levels high, with columns, faux windows, and a crown-shaped tholos in the centre. The Monastery is just as spectacular as the Treasury, but perhaps not as famous because it hasn't had the same Hollywood treatment.

Petra also has Roman and Byzantine ruins from when those empires controlled the city towards the end of its history, but much of the site is still to be uncovered. The official size of the archaeological park is about 260 square kilometres (100 square miles) and only 15 per cent of it has been excavated. If you were to try to follow Indiana Jones into the Treasury to find the Holy Grail, you would realise that it's just a small room beyond the façade. But perhaps there is still an archaeological holy grail to be found here somewhere.

**01.** The tomb known as the Monastery, which is hidden up a hill from the main part of the city **02.** Looking out across the dry desert landscape that surrounds Petra **03.** Camels wait in front of the Treasury, the most famous tomb within the ancient city

The tomb known as the Monastery was carved into the rock at Petra in the 1st century CE

01

# Ayutthaya

### *Thailand* (Inscribed 1991)

It's said that, in the 1700s, Ayutthaya was the largest city in the world, taking the mantle from Beijing in the period before London grew to the peak of its imperial and industrial power. Ayutthaya was the second capital (after Sukhothai) of the powerful Siamese Kingdom, which controlled much of the land in Southeast Asia at the time. But it also had the benefit of being an island in the middle of three large rivers in the Chao Phraya Basin, offering a strong defensive position. These rivers connected to sea ports, giving access to the Bay of Bengal and the South China Sea, making the city an epicentre of global maritime trade. Bringing together merchants from Europe, the Middle East, and other parts of Asia, it was home to up to one million people.

Founded in 1351, Ayutthaya grew quickly into a monumental capital based on a grid pattern with roads, moats, and canals – leading to its nickname The Venice of the East (obviously because of the canals, although the crowds of foreigners would also have made the name appropriate). The streets would have been full of bustling markets, including local traders trying to sell deer skins and wood from the forests. The water for the canals came from the three rivers around the city, which were intended to be defensive. However, nothing was able to stop the Burmese armies that invaded the city in 1767.

What still remains from the sacking by the Burmese are the large compounds of the temples and monasteries, with their incredible reliquary towers known as prang. At the temple called Wat Chaiwatthanaram, for instance, there's a central 35-metre-high (115-foot) tower with a corn-cob shape that represents the sacred Mount Meru. Around it are smaller spires called chedis that were once decorated with sculptures depicting scenes from the life of Buddha. At the Wat Mahathat temple, stone columns mark out the central path that led between the towers, although the most photographed spot is the head of a Buddha statue that's now encompassed by the roots of a banyan tree.

The statue is a bit like all the ruins of the ancient city, which are now enveloped by modern Ayutthaya, busy motorbike-congested streets passing right by the old monasteries. With a population now of just 50,000 people, it's a fragment of the great royal capital it once was, but the beautiful historic towers

rising amongst the drab commercial buildings of today still evoke the grandeur of a global metropolis. And, in some ways, it lives on in the third capital of the Siamese Kingdom, Bangkok, which used Ayutthaya as the inspiration for its development.

**01.** The remains of the temples in Ayutthaya are at least 600 years old **02.** The Buddha head surrounded by the roots of a banyan tree at Wat Mahathat **03.** A large prang (tower) at the Wat Ratchaburana temple

# Ancient civilisations

Definitions can get a little murky (what's the difference between a civilisation and being civilised, for instance?), but across the world, unconnected by era or geography, different cultures developed into empires independent of each other. At first, by domesticating animals and controlling agriculture, they transitioned from hunter-gatherer lifestyles, leading to the development of mathematics, writing, transportation, engineering and military. In later years, they constructed metropolises and spread across continents. Some empires became iconic while others faded into relative obscurity. But from the jungles to the deserts, this non-exhaustive collection of World Heritage Sites shows there are many ways for travellers to discover the countless dynasties that rose and fell over the millennia.

I think it's fair to say that it was in the Fertile Crescent of Mesopotamia that we saw the first major cities within societies. In Iraq, we can incredibly still find some structures from probably the world's first civilisation, Sumer, which developed about 6000 years ago. There are quite a few remnants from three cities — **Uruk**, **Ur**, and **Tell Eridu** — but the most impressive is the reconstructed series of layered terraces and access staircases that make up the Ziggurat of Ur, a huge temple complex that looks like an early prototype of a pyramid.

On the coast of Peru, about 600 kilometres (373 miles) from Machu Picchu (*see* p. 228), the first civilisation of either American continent was built by the Caral at **Caral-Supe** more than 5000 years ago. Astonishingly, there are six relatively well-preserved pyramids at the site, which were built around the same time as the Giza Pyramids (*see* p. 222), although much smaller. In other parts of Peru, there are still the remains of other civilisations — the Chavin at **Chavin de Huantar** from the 15th century BCE, with artwork that inspired

| | |
|---|---|
| 2600 BCE | **Caral-Supe**<br>**(Inscribed 2009)** |
| 2551–2528 BCE | The Giza Pyramids<br>*(see p. 222)* |
| 2500 BCE | **Moenjodaro**<br>**(Inscribed 1980)** |
| 15th century BCE | **Chavin de Huantar**<br>**(Inscribed 1985)** |
| 1300 BCE | **Yin Xu**<br>**(Inscribed 2006)** |
| 5th century BCE | Nazca Lines<br>*(see p. 136)* |
| 4th–3rd century BCE | **Uruk, Ur, and Tell Eridu**<br>**(Inscribed 2016)** |
| 1st–8th century CE | **Religious monuments and**<br>**sculptures of San Agustín**<br>**(Inscribed 1995)** |
| 1st–6th century CE | **Teotihuacan**<br>**(Inscribed 1987)** |
| 4th century CE | **Fort Samaipata**<br>**(Inscribed 1998)** |
| 400–900 CE | **Tiwanaku**<br>**(Inscribed 2000)** |
| 600–900 CE | **Underground tombs of Tierradentro**<br>**(inscribed 1995)** |
| 700 CE | **Temples at Xochicalco**<br>**(Inscribed 1999)** |
| 7th–13th century CE | **El Tajin**<br>**(Inscribed 1992)** |
| 14th–16th Century CE | **Tenochtitlan**<br>**(Mexico City inscribed 1987)** |
| 15th century CE | **Chan Chan**<br>**(Inscribed 1986)** |
| 15th Century CE | Machu Picchu<br>*(see p. 228)* |

Pablo Picasso; the mysterious Nazca and their **Nazca Lines** (*see* p. 136) in the desert from the 5th century BCE; and the Chimor with the mud city of **Chan Chan** from the 15th century CE that was invaded by the Incas.

In Bolivia, you'll find the striking carved hill of **Fort Samaipata** from the Mojocoyas as early as the 4th century CE; and the ancient city of **Tiwanaku** with the remains of an enormous pyramid built by the Tiwanaku culture. In Colombia, there is the necropolis with 7-metre-tall (23-foot) humanoid sculptures from the 2000-year-old **San Agustín** culture; while elsewhere there are the decorated underground tombs from the **Tierradentro** culture.

In Central America, the Aztec's capital **Tenochtitlan** forms the base of Mexico City (*see* p. 58). Before the Aztec Empire, other civilisations made their marks in Mexico at the huge city of **Teotihuacan** (named for the culture) from the 1st to 6th centuries CE, with its iconic 65-metre-high (213-foot) Pyramid of the Sun; the temples at the **Xochicalco** (also named for the culture), from about 700 CE; and the remarkable collection of palaces, temples, and pyramids at **El Tajín**, which flourished from the 7th to 13th centuries CE at the centre of the Classic Veracruz culture.

Around 2600 BCE, the Harappan Civilisation emerged in the Indus Valley, around modern-day India and Pakistan, it's best represented by the ancient city of **Moenjodaro** in northern Pakistan, which was founded about 4500 years ago. The large urban centre with houses built from mud bricks might have had a population of 40,000 living in it, while a citadel about 12 metres (39 feet) above the city had assembly halls, public baths, and a palace-like structure with room for about 5000 people.

The Erlitou Culture emerged in China from about 1900 BCE. No archaeological sites from exactly this period have been found but an ancient capital city called **Yin Xu** that emerged several centuries later has been discovered. While just the foundations of the royal palace and other buildings remain, the artefacts found here are quite incredible, especially the 'oracle bones' where prayers were written onto animal bones (mainly turtle or cow) and then burned to see how they cracked. More than 100,000 of these bones have been found at Yin Xu, revealing the desires of kings to win battles ... or just to stop a toothache.

Chan Chan in Peru **Previous** Ruins of Chavin de Huantar, Peru

# Love at first site

What would life be without love? It warms, it inspires, it leads to great acts of devotion, and it's celebrated in music, poetry, art, literature, and even architecture. We have always loved, which is why we can see the strongest of human emotion play out often in some of the most famous UNESCO World Heritage Sites.

There's the majestic mausoleum of India's Taj Mahal (*see* p. 252), built by a Mughal emperor in the 17th century as a demonstration of his love for his late wife; the ancient city of Troy (*see* p. 264), that legend says was laid to siege for 10 years because of the love between Paris and Helen; and the romance that's found in the elegant Austrian city of Salzburg (*see* p. 268), where music hangs in the air.

Ah, but what's in a name? That which we call a rose, by any other name would smell as sweet, right? Verona (*see* p. 256) may be known as the setting for Shakespeare's *Romeo and Juliet* but its collection of history is inspiring in its own ways. Just as the Singapore Botanic Gardens (*see* p. 260) is one of the city's most popular wedding venues, but is significant for its scientific research into tropical plants.

These sites of love and romance do pull at the heart, but they also exercise the mind and tell us the stories and legends behind the passion, showing yet again why visiting World Heritage Sites is such a rewarding experience.

# Taj Mahal

## *India* (Inscribed 1983)

When the favourite wife of Mughal Emperor Shah Jahan died during childbirth in 1631 CE, he was inconsolable. Mumtaz Mahal had been his one true love, and now she was gone. After a year of mourning in private, Shah Jahan turned his attention to honouring her with a mausoleum as beautiful, elegant, and gracious as she was. As a tribute to Mumtaz Mahal, the emperor built her an eternal home greater than anyone had ever seen, one that would carry her name forever – the Taj Mahal.

Love comes at a price, though, and it's said the Taj Mahal had a build cost of about a billion US dollars in today's terms. (And, if you believe the apocryphal stories, it also cost the eyes of the architect and the hands of the masons, maimed by Shah Jahan so they could never build anything better.) It took 16 years to construct, with estimates that about 22,000 labourers and 1000 elephants were put to work. Jade was brought from China, turquoise from Tibet, sapphire from Sri Lanka, and all these gems were intricately inlaid into detailed patterns on white marble that was transported from about 300 kilometres (186 miles) away. Shah Jahan achieved his dream, a mausoleum that befitted his wife, but also one that captured the heart of the world.

You may have heard people try to tell you the Taj Mahal is not as big in person as you'd expect. Don't believe them. The mausoleum is 68 metres high (223 feet) and sits 5 metres

01

(16 feet) above the ground on an elevated square platform, 100 metres (328 feet) along each side, with a minaret on each corner. Even though it is just a small part of the garden compound that leads to it, with a canal of water stretching from the main gate to the platform, the Taj Mahal is imposing and constantly draws your eye towards it.

I visited at both sunrise and sunset (something I would recommend, if you're able to) and it's remarkable to see how the colour of the building changes at different times of the day. From grey to pink first thing in the morning, an ivory white during the day, and a bright orange as dusk approaches. There is symbolism in the design, with the symmetry throughout the whole site representing harmony; red and white stone being a reference to social classes of the time; and imagery of plants a nod to both paradise and the emperor's own political standing.

The Taj Mahal created a new style of Islamic architecture that spread across the Muslim world, but none of the buildings it inspired have ever overtaken the reputation of the original. It's just too perfect already, with an emotional dynamism in the interplay of the curves and the straight lines, the shadows and the light, the arches and the domes. You feel it when you first see the mausoleum through the main gate, as it gets closer when you walk down the paths in the garden, and as you step up onto the platform and then go inside.

In the centre of the Taj Mahal's interior is the cenotaph of Mumtaz Mahal, and on the western side of it is Shah Jahan's cenotaph, the only asymmetrical feature in the whole complex. But they are together, side by side for eternity, in the symbol of their love.

01. Sunset at the Taj Mahal, which appears to change colour throughout the day 02. A long water feature stretches from the main gate to the front of the Taj Mahal mausoleum 03. Large gardens within the site are connected by paths between the grass

A couple leans against the shining marble of the Taj Mahal

# Verona

## *Italy* (Inscribed 2000)

'There is no world without Verona's walls,' Shakespeare wrote as he built the climax to one of the world's most famous plays, the tale of a Capulet and a Montague – a pair of star-cross'd lovers – who discovered that violent delights do indeed have violent ends. But while *Romeo and Juliet* ultimately ends in tragedy, it is the power of their love that has made it such an enduring story.

The narrative is timeless – love will often come in inconvenient forms – and Shakespeare (probably intentionally) never reveals in what period of time the events occur. Yet most academics agree *Romeo and Juliet* was probably set in the 1300s, a time when Verona was ruled by powerful families, rather than royalty or emperors. This was the era when the city flourished under the Scaliger family, who built many of the monuments that led the city to become a World Heritage Site hundreds of years later.

The focus of the architecture from the Scaliger period is on the Piazza delle Erbe, particularly the Casa dei Mercanti (House of Merchants), a two-storey building with battlements on the top and a large porch with arches on the ground level. Around the piazza are other important landmarks, such as the imposing Palazzo Maffei in Baroque style, and the Mazzanti Houses that have frescoes painted on the exterior of the upper levels.

Piazza delle Erbe was the city's forum during Ancient Rome, where people would shop at the markets and discuss civic business. There are

still markets today, but not much remains from the Roman period. However, you only have to go a few hundred metres to find the best legacy of that time: the Arena di Verona. Built in 30 CE, it is a magnificent amphitheatre large enough to once have held 30,000 spectators. It's still used today for regular performances (I saw a lively version of the opera *Carmen* there once), but seats about half as many as it did in ancient times.

At the Piazza dei Signori are more impressive civic buildings, most of them elegant palazzi (palaces) from the Renaissance period. As you wander through the streets of Verona's historic centre, you'll find even more landmarks from the period between the 15th and 18th centuries when the city was part of the Republic of Venice. There are more than two millennia of landmarks showing the rich history of Verona. It's why I think it's quite unfortunate that so many visitors to the city head straight for a tourist trap called Casa di Giulietta (Juliet's

House), which is just an ordinary (albeit 13th-century) residence with a balcony looking over a courtyard – reminiscent of the scene in *Romeo and Juliet* when the young lover asks, 'wherefore art thou Romeo?' – and pay to have their photo taken. This commercialisation has little authenticity and distracts from the real heritage. Never was a story of more woe than this of Juliet and her cameo.

**01.** The Mazzanti Houses are painted with frescoes on the upper levels **02.** A bridge across the Adige River **03.** Across the city, a range of buildings show architecture styles spanning hundreds of years

# Westminster Abbey

## *United Kingdom* (Inscribed 1987)

There were only about 2200 people sitting in Westminster Abbey in 2011 when Kate Middleton walked down the aisle towards Prince William, but an estimated billion people around the world may have felt like they were there, holding their breath as they watched the royal wedding on television. Any royal wedding is a big event, but one held in a 'royal church' adds more pomp to the circumstance, and this was certainly a spectacle.

The nuptials of William and Kate in 2011 is the latest royal wedding to have been held at Westminster Abbey, but there have only been 16 throughout history, the first being King Henry I's to Matilda of Scotland in 1100 (in the Norman church). Recent weddings include those of Queen Elizabeth II and Prince Philip in 1947, the Queen's sister Princess Margaret and Antony Armstrong-Jones in 1960, the Queen and Prince Philip's daughter Princess Anne and Captain Mark Phillips in 1973, and the Queen and Prince Philip's son Prince Andrew and Sarah Ferguson in 1986. (The 1981 wedding of Prince Charles and Lady Diana Spencer was at London's St Paul's Cathedral.)

The first church was founded on the site in 960 CE but construction of the current building didn't begin until the 13th century, with the two distinctive towers rising on either side of the entrance not added until the 18th century. Westminster Abbey has been part of British history's pageantry for a millennium, the

01

location for every coronation since 1066, for the funerals of many royals, including Princess Diana in 1997, and as the burial site for 30 kings and queens.

Visiting, you'll discover that the large interior you've seen in televised weddings is even more cavernous in person, filled with hundreds of small details like sculptures, stained-glass windows, dedications to notable writers, and even the coronation chair. But if you feel the building alone doesn't have enough gravitas, there's more in the audio-guide's deep-voiced narration by actor Jeremy Irons.

If you were hoping to one day get married at Westminster Abbey yourself, unfortunately the odds are not favourable. The only people allowed to hold weddings here are members of the Royal Family, members of the Order of the Bath and their children, and anyone who lives in the Abbey's precincts. However, you may be able to get married in the 14th-century St Margaret's Church, which is on the Abbey's grounds and also part of the World Heritage Site. The site also includes the Palace of Westminster, home to the Houses of Parliament, but with all the politicians there's probably no love lost there.

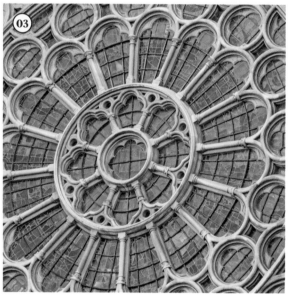

**01.** The two towers at the front of Westminster Abbey were not added until the 18th century **02.** Statues of 20th-century Christian martyrs Janani Luwum, Grand Duchess Elizabeth of Russia, Martin Luther King Jr, Oscar Romero, and Dietrich Bonhoeffer **03.** Small details, like the stained-glass window on the façade, mean you can spend hours exploring the church

# Singapore Botanic Gardens

## *Singapore* (Inscribed 2015)

In the centre of a frenetic metropolis, the Singapore Botanic Gardens are a quiet oasis from the bustling streets. The tropical green breath of nature is one of just three botanic gardens that have been named as World Heritage Sites (the others are the Botanical Garden of Padua in Italy, and the Royal Botanic Gardens Kew in the UK). It is a symbol of love for the city, a host for weddings and a home for the eternal union of flowers.

When Singapore chose a national flower in 1981, it turned to an orchid that had been created as a hybrid about a century earlier – a sort of floral love story, if you will. The Vanda Miss Joaquim – named after the keen gardener who grew it, Agnes Joaquim – was chosen not just because of its delicate mauve and violet petals, but because its hardiness and resilience reflect the Singaporean spirit. Not long after Miss Joaquim created the flower, the Director of the Singapore Botanic Gardens, HN Ridley, introduced it to the world in an 1893 edition of *Gardeners' Chronicle*, writing, 'It is a very lovely plant, and is, I think, a great improvement on both the parents, beautiful as they are'. The Vanda Miss Joaquim is still one of the prized possessions of the Botanic Gardens' National Orchid Garden, which has about 600 species on display, with special notes next to those that have been renamed in honour of the heads of state they were given to.

For many Singaporeans, the Botanic Gardens is embraced for its aesthetics – paths leading past lakes and waterfalls, soft green lawns for picnics, sculptures set amongst flower beds. It's become a popular location for weddings, especially for photos at the bandstand, which was built from tropical hardwoods in 1860 for military bands to play concerts twice a month.

The Singapore Botanic Gardens was added to the World Heritage List for its significance as a scientific institution. Founded in 1859 when the city was under British colonial rule, it was used to research tropical flora and horticulture, and was critical in the development of plantation rubber across the Malay Peninsula. Singapore is often called the City of Gardens, but it's for more than just the green spaces – it's also a nod to the importance this particular garden played in the city's economic and cultural history.

# The Singapore Botanic Gardens was added to the World Heritage List for its significance as a scientific institution.

**01.** The bandstand was built in 1860 for military bands to play concerts **02.** The Vanda Miss Joaquim, an orchid that is the national flower of Singapore **03.** The Singapore Botanic Gardens offers a tranquil retreat from the hectic city

# World Heritage proposals

Before a wedding, comes a very important event – a proposal. For some couples this may just be a casual conversation over a meal, but for others it can be almost as much of an extravaganza as the wedding itself. Down on one knee, popping the question, popping the champagne. It's a big moment.

A lot of people like to find a special location befitting of this memorable step in their lives, and it's common to even plan an international trip around it. There have been several analyses of thousands of social media posts using popular proposal hashtags to try to determine where some of the most common places are to ask for someone's hand in marriage. Perhaps it should be no surprise that the majority of the top proposal spots are World Heritage Sites.

The most popular World Heritage Site for a proposal is, unsurprisingly, the **Eiffel Tower** in Paris, one of the most romantic cities in the world and a famous spot for lovers for decades. Next on the list is not quite as obvious — the **Grand Canyon** in the USA (*see* p. 174). Hopefully the enormous chasm down the middle is not a bad omen for the marriage.

There are three locations on the list that are within the World Heritage Site of the **Historic Centre of Rome** (*see* p. 224): the Colosseum, the Spanish Steps, and the Trevi Fountain, each iconic in their own way, although the gladiatorial arena seems a slightly strange spot for a romantic gesture. The **Sydney Opera House** (*see* p. 128), also apparently a popular proposal site, offers a stunning background for the engagement photo.

In fact, by analysing social media there's probably a bias towards proposals that were intentionally done in scenic locations. It's presumably why the sites also include **Lake Louise** in Canada, and **Table Mountain** in South Africa. But it's nice to also see on the list the **Taj Mahal** (*see* p. 252), not just a picturesque background, but a tribute to a happy loving marriage.

# *Perhaps it should be no surprise that the majority of the top proposal spots are World Heritage Sites.*

The Eiffel Tower, Paris, France **Inset** The Trevi Fountain, Rome, Italy

# Troy

## *Turkey* (Inscribed 1998)

She was 'the face that launched a thousand ships'. She was also known as Helen of Sparta, who became Helen of Troy – perhaps the daughter of Zeus. And she was enamoured with the young Prince Paris (after an intervention by Aphrodite, the Goddess of Love), who took her to his homeland, sparking the 10-year Trojan War that would end only because of a huge wooden horse. If we have learned anything from ancient history, it's that Greek mythology is never boring.

There's disagreement among historians on whether the story of the Trojan War is truth or legend. It was said to have occurred around the 13th century BCE and was the focus of Homer's famous works, *The Iliad*, and, to some degree, *The Odyssey*, but there's little evidence of its veracity. Even Troy itself was thought by many to be fictional, although believers continued to search for its location for thousands of years, with the quest taking on a new fervour from the 16th century. A site in Turkey was identified as a possibility in 1822 by the Scottish

01

journalist Charles Maclaren, but it wasn't until archaeological work beginning about 40 years later that it was confirmed as the ancient city of Troy.

What excavations of the site found was at least nine versions of Troy over more than three millennia, each destroyed by fire or earthquakes, with the next city just built on top of levelled rubble. From a small settlement in about 3000 BCE, it gradually turned into a large city with 5-metre-high (16-foot) limestone walls around it, and a central fortified citadel with grand houses on terraces within the walls. Did one of those houses belong to Paris? Finally the site was occupied by the Romans, who renamed it Ilium and built temples and a theatre, the ruins of which you can still see today.

Of course, everything you see at Troy when you visit now is in ruins. The excavations have focused on a relatively small area, no more than 300 metres (984 feet) across, but they have uncovered a huge amount of the city's history:

temples, shrines, houses, parts of the citadel. You can see the terraces in the centre, the main streets, piles of columns that would once have stood proud. Although it was lost for eons, Troy was a powerful force in this region for a long time.

If Troy existed, as we now know it did, perhaps that means the Trojan War did occur in the way the ancient literature describes it. There are certainly some signs within the ruins that suggest major conflict around that time. And that could mean that Helen did exist, perhaps not the daughter of a god, but quite possibly the most beautiful woman in the world – for whom it was worth starting a war.

01. An aerial view of the archaeological site of Troy 02. An ancient theatre shows Troy would've once been a wealthy city 03. Most of the city is still in ruins or is buried and yet to be excavated

# Pafos

## *Cyprus* (Inscribed 1980)

According to Ancient Greek mythology, Aphrodite, the Goddess of Love, emerged naked from the water and onto a beach in Cyprus. She had just been created from the foam of the sea caused by Cronus castrating his father Uranus and throwing his genitals into the water. The wind had blown her here, to her spiritual home.

Regardless of whether the story is true or legend, Aphrodite was born near Pafos on the island of Cyprus ... at least, the idea of her was. Not far from the coast, at the Sanctuary

of Aphrodite at Kouklia, are the architectural remains of the original temple of the cult that worshipped her, built in the 12th century BCE. Although, what we know as Aphrodite today was a long evolution, with evidence that non-humanoid fertility deities had been worshipped here for about 3000 years before the temple was built on the site.

Homer mentioned the Sanctuary of Aphrodite in *The Odyssey* in the 8th century BCE, one of the factors in the complex becoming a popular pilgrimage destination in ancient times. Visitors today will possibly find no other tourists at the archaeological site but, along with some remaining blocks from the original temple, there are ruins of the accommodation and businesses built for all the pilgrims thousands

# Visitors today will possibly find no other tourists at the archaeological site

wealthy residents who had decorated their floors with sophisticated mosaics showing scenes from legends, of history, and daily life. Many of these artworks have been well restored, colours vibrant and details clear, and they are a highlight of a visit to Pafos, just metres from the large modern hotels with tourists who emerge from a swim in the same waters where Aphrodite was created.

of years ago. There's also a large blob of black basalt that was once worshipped as an ancient representation of a goddess, but is the antithesis of the delicate feminine imagery of Aphrodite or Botticelli's Venus (the Roman counterpart of Aphrodite) that it evolved into.

The World Heritage Site at Pafos also includes the ancient city of Kato Pafos, where the inhabitants around the sanctuary at Kouklia moved in the 4th century BCE because it had a better harbour. Within the large archaeological park are the ruins of dozens of houses of

**01.** Conservators are constantly working to restore and maintain the mosaics at Kato Pafos **02.** The original site of the temple of the Cult of Aphrodite **03.** Mosaics at Kato Pafos are from the floors of the houses of wealthy residents

# Salzburg

*Austria* (Inscribed 1996)

In the sound of music, we hear the sound of joy, of sadness, of anger, of peace. But most of all, we hear the sound of love. In the beautiful World Heritage city of Salzburg, music floats through the air and spreads its love with it.

You may hear it from the mouths of tourists. For decades, the Austrian city has captured the hearts of fans of the Academy Award–winning movie *The Sound of Music* (1965), much of which was set and filmed here. Tour guides not only lead their guests to locations featured in

the film, they often play the songs on a speaker, encouraging everyone to sing – perhaps a rendition of *Do-Re-Mi* at the Pegasus Fountain in Mirabell Gardens, for instance.

You may hear the music of the city's love in the works of one of its most famous residents: Wolfgang Amadeus Mozart. From *Eine kleine Nachtmusik* (A little serenade), through to operas like *The Magic Flute* and *The Marriage of Figaro*, Mozart's moving movements are timeless. The 18th-century composer is even recognised in Salzburg's official World Heritage Site listing, when it makes mention of the city attracting artists from across the continent, declaring: 'This meeting-point of northern and southern Europe perhaps sparked the genius of Salzburg's most famous son.' His birthplace

01

and his residence, once normal houses, are now museums that offer an insight into the city's heritage as much as the musician's life. And you may hear it, as I did when I visited, wafting out from choirs through the open doors of one of the city's 27 churches, including the magnificent Salzburg Cathedral where Mozart was baptised.

Salzburg became a wealthy city from its salt extraction industry (Salzburg literally means 'Salt Castle') and the profits brought artists and architects from across Europe, who built an exquisite historic centre. On the main hill, the hulking Hohensalzburg Fortress, founded in the 11th century, is one of the largest medieval castles on the continent. Below, the Salzach River is cradled by the Old Town, a handsome collection of Baroque avenues and alleys.

Hellbrunn Palace, 5 kilometres (3 miles) out of town, is also part of the World Heritage Site. Another Baroque masterpiece, it was built by

the Prince-Archbishop of Salzburg in 1619 as a day residence for the summer period. The highlight here is the Trick Fountains, which you can visit on a tour, but expect surprise jets of water and other high jinks that were designed to entertain 17th-century guests (and 21st-century ones too, apparently). In the grounds of Hellbrunn Palace, you'll also find the gazebo used to film the song *Sixteen Going On Seventeen* in *The Sound of Music* – and, yes, more singing.

**01.** The view across the centre of Salzburg from Hohensalzburg Fortress **02.** Salzburg Cathedral is just one of 27 churches in the city **03.** Cyclists on a *The Sound of Music* tour on the outskirts of the historic centre

# Valparaíso

## *Chile* (Inscribed 2003)

The Chilean city of Valparaíso is on the coast, just 120 kilometres (74.5 miles) from the country's inland capital, Santiago, and as soon as you arrive you can feel the difference in the cool sea breezes. They bring with them a breath of energy, filling the colourful city with life – for Valparaíso, a city of culture, has a lyrical rhythm.

The Chilean poet, Pablo Neruda, lived in Valparaíso and wrote about his city, describing it as crazy and dishevelled. But he used these words lovingly, and was enamoured with the nonsense and surprise that he constantly found in the colours and organic layout. You can almost imagine him shouting his poems out across the natural amphitheatre that is created by the central port, low-lying commercial centre, and ring of residential hills.

Neruda's house sits atop one of these hills, watching the mess of buildings below. His home is now a museum and, visiting it, you can see why the Nobel Prize–winning poet chose this coastal city as one of his bases. It reflects the passion found in his most famous collection of poetry, *Veinte poemas de amor y una canción desesperada* (Twenty Love Poems and a Song of Despair), but also the melancholy. Neruda wasn't writing about heritage sites. He was 19 and was writing about women. Yet, like most poetry, the meaning comes from the reader. Valparaíso was the most important merchant port on the western side of South America at the end of the 1800s but, just a few decades after it rose to prominence, the Panama Canal opened and it lost its strategic position.

## 02

To feel the beat of the city, you need to hit the streets, but it's easy to get lost in Valparaíso. The roads wind up and down the hills with no apparent forethought, following the contours of the terrain or the needs of the residents. The suburbs flow in from the coastline and up the knobs of the hills, filling every bit of land stretching from the sea to the ragged skyline. And each house is painted a different colour, no two adjacent buildings the same – a panoramic kaleidoscope. I was told by a local guide that this is because the owners used leftover paint from ships at the dock, whatever colour was available, regardless of whether it was their preference. The vibrancy created here more than a century ago remains, celebrated by people coming from across the world again, who will fall in love and take a long time to forget.

# To feel the beat of the city, you need to hit the streets, but it's easy to get lost in Valparaíso.

**01.** The colourful buildings of the city start in the centre and spread across the hills **02.** The streets (and staircases) of Valparaíso are covered in artwork **03.** One of the historic funiculars that takes passengers up the hills in the city centre

# A love of heritage

In this book, I have written a lot about the people who created the places that have become World Heritage Sites – emperors and architects, communities and artists. But we also need to pay tribute to the heritage managers of these sites, who have restored ruins to glory, fought bureaucracy to protect history, and maintain them today so that we can still see them ourselves.

After I visited the ruins of the ancient city of Aphrodisias in Turkey in 2012, I wrote as the introduction to a story: 'It's all about love, isn't it? And at the ancient temple dedicated to Aphrodite, the love goddess, you can feel it all around you. Not just in the ethereal sense, but in the practical. For it was the love of history that saw Turkish archaeologist Kenan Erim dedicate his life to uncovering the story of Aphrodisias. It became his second home for 30 years and, now buried there, his eternal resting place.'

That was not long after I had started my campaign to visit every World Heritage Site and, since then, I have been fortunate enough to meet a lot of the people who have chosen to protect and research these locations. It's more than a job for them. It's a calling and a passion. They see their role as more important than just the years they spend doing it; it is a part of a much longer process of safeguarding heritage for generation after generation.

Almost as important as those who protect these sites are those who visit them because, in some ways, heritage only exists if people are aware of it. We can protect the physical elements of a site, but they have no meaning unless we see them and understand them. A brick is just a brick until it becomes part of a story. To love heritage is to give it value.

Many of the natural World Heritage Sites covered in this book were here for millions of years before humans left their first footsteps on them. But when it comes to the cultural sites of our own creation, often we have been forgetting them for longer than they existed. Short periods of significance in history can be significant forever in our collective narrative. By protecting them – and by visiting them – we show our love of the world, and we give these sites new life. The word 'heritage' has connotations of history, but by exploring so many of these World Heritage Sites, I have come to realise that heritage is just a piece of who we are today. You can't appreciate the present without the past.

*Almost as important as those who protect these sites are those who visit them because, in some ways, heritage only exists if people are aware of it.*

Aphrodisias in Turkey

# Index

# About the author

Michael Turtle has been a full-time travel writer and blogger for more than a decade, visiting more than 75 countries (and going through a few passports). Michael's interest in the culture and history of the places he visits inspired him to start seeking out World Heritage Sites and he has been to more than 320 of them on his journeys. He's even worked for UNESCO to produce stories and photos about some of the sites.

Michael runs the popular travel blog, Time Travel Turtle, which inspires people to explore the world by seeing destinations through their heritage, people, and modern culture. He is also a weekly contributor to *The Canberra Times*. His articles and photos have won numerous awards, including the 2020 Best Travel Blog from the Australian Society of Travel Writers. Before he set off into the world with his backpack, Michael had worked as a national television and radio reporter at the Australian Broadcast Company (ABC), a newsreader at Triple J radio, and entertainment producer at Channel Seven in Australia.

# Resources

timetravelturtle.com/unesco-world-heritage-list

whc.unesco.org

whc.unesco.org/en/criteria

whc.unesco.org/en/extractive-industries

whc.unesco.org/en/marine-programme

unesco.org/new/en/culture/gender-and-culture/gender-equality-and-culture/the-report

clc.org.au/files/pdf/Sammy_Wilson_statement_on_Uluru_climb.pdf

pangea.stanford.edu/news/radiation-exposed-corals-bikini-atoll-may-hold-insights-cancer

icomos.org/images/ICOMOS_Second_discussion_paper_Sites_associated_with_memories_of_recent_conflicts.pdf

britishmuseum.org/about-us/british-museum-story/objects-news/parthenon-sculptures/parthenon-sculptures-trustees

# Photo credits

All images are © Michael Turtle with the exception of the following:

Front cover, spine and endpapers: iStock; pp. 11 (inset), 32, 33 (top), 59 (top), 63 (top), 68, 70, 71 (top), 76, 77, 83 (bottom), 87, 90, 91, 103, 126, 133 (top), 140, 141 (bottom), 167 (top), 168, 169 (bottom), 170–171, 179 (inset), 187 (bottom), 198, 199 (bottom), 215, 237 (bottom), 238, 263 (bottom), 265 (top) iStock; p. 11 Unsplash/Mike Cummings; p. 18 ID1974 / Shutterstock.com; pp. 19, 22, 23, 24, 33 (bottom), 36, 43, 58, 59 (bottom), 62, 63 (bottom), 71 (bottom), 83 (top), 97 (inset), 102, 103 (bottom), 105, 106, 107 (bottom), 119, 125, 130, 134, 141 (top), 148, 149, 151, 156, 158, 166, 175 (bottom), 179, 187 (inset), 188, 189 (bottom), 203 (inset), 206, 207 (top), 236, 237 (top), 239, 259 (bottom), 261, 264, 265 (bottom) Shutterstock.com; p. 24 javarman / Shutterstock.com; p. 38 Unsplash/16 degree; p. 39 (top) Unsplash/ Tomas Williams; p. 39 (bottom) Unsplash/Pierpaolo Lucarelli; p. 42 Unsplash/Timo Volz; p. 43 CK Travels / Shutterstock.com; pp. 52, 52 (top) Unsplash/ Vladimir Haltakov; p. 53 (bottom) Takashi Images / Shutterstock.com; p. 59 (bottom) Eddy Galeotti / Shutterstock.com; p. 69 (top) S KUMAR KARAMANA / Shutterstock.com; p. 69 (bottom) travelwild / Shutterstock.com; p. 71 (bottom) rafastockbr / Shutterstock.com; p. 80 Unsplash/ Polina Kuzovkova; p. 81 (top) Unsplash/ Miguel Andrade Guerrero; p. 81 (bottom) javier gonzalez leyva / Shutterstock.com; p. 86 Unsplash/Robert Bye; pp. 97, 145 (bottom), 157, 184, 185, 199 (top), 203, 207 (bottom), 218 Alamy; p. 107 Unsplash/Dan Wechter; p. 118 Unsplash/ Jonathan Velasquez; p. 119 (top) Alessandro Colle / Shutterstock.com; p. 119 (bottom) Alina Zamogilnykh / Shutterstock.com; p. 127 (top) Unsplash/ Juan Manuel Aguilar; p. 127 (bottom) Unsplash/Priyanka Puvvada; p. 129 (bottom) Unsplash/Angela Matijczak; p. 130 Alan Tan Photography / Shutterstock.com; p. 131 (top) Unsplash/Iam Os; p. 131 (bottom) Unsplash/Tomas Nozina; p. 135 Unsplash/ Stephanie Morcinek; pp. 144, 145 The Havanna Vanuatu; p. 148 (bottom) Mirko Kuzmanovic / Shutterstock.com; p. 151 (bottom) Buffy1982/Shutterstock.com; p. 167 (bottom) Unsplash/Ben Lowe; p. 169 (top) Unsplash/Jason Zhao; p. 174 Unsplash/ Aaron Bookout; p. 175 (top) Unsplash/Jura Greyling; p. 189 (top) Unsplash/Agnieszka Mordaunt; p. 190 Unsplash/Misha Levko; p. 191 (top) Biro Iosif Ionut / Shutterstock.com; p. 260 happycreator / Shutterstock.com; p. 261 (bottom) Marek Poplawski / Shutterstock.com; p. 263 Unsplash/ Fabrizio Verrecchia.

Published in 2021 by Hardie Grant Travel, a division of
Hardie Grant Publishing

Hardie Grant Travel (Melbourne)
Wurundjeri Country
Building 1, 658 Church Street
Richmond, Victoria 3121

Hardie Grant Travel (Sydney)
Gadigal Country
Level 7, 45 Jones Street
Ultimo, NSW 2007

www.hardiegrant.com/au/travel

All rights reserved. No part of this publication may be reproduced, stored in a
retrieval system or transmitted in any form by any means, electronic, mechanical,
photocopying, recording or otherwise, without the prior written permission of the
publishers and copyright holders.

The moral rights of the author have been asserted.

Copyright text © Michael Turtle 2021
Copyright concept, maps and design © Hardie Grant Publishing 2021

Maps in this publication were made with Natural Earth @ naturalearthdata.com

A catalogue record for this
book is available from the
National Library of Australia

Hardie Grant acknowledges the Traditional Owners of the Country on which we
work, the Wurundjeri people of the Kulin Nation and the Gadigal people of the
Eora Nation, and recognises their continuing connection to the land, waters and
culture. We pay our respects to their Elders past, present and emerging.

Great World Wonders
ISBN 9781741177312

10 9 8 7 6 5 4 3 2 1

**Publisher**
Melissa Kayser

**Cartographer**
Emily Maffei

**Project editor**
Megan Cuthbert

**Design**
Hannah Janzen

**Editor**
Alice Barker

**Typesetting**
Megan Ellis

**Editorial assistance**
Rosanna Dutson

**Index**
Max McMaster

**Proofreader**
Judith Bamber

Colour reproduction by Megan Ellis and Splitting Image Colour Studio

Printed and bound in China by LEO Paper Products LTD.

The paper this book is printed on is certified against the
Forest Stewardship Council® Standards and other
sources. FSC® promotes environmentally responsible,
socially beneficial and economically viable management
of the world's forests.

**Publisher's Note:** Every effort has been made to ensure that the information
in this book is accurate at the time of going to press. The publisher welcomes
information and suggestions for correction or improvement.